Extraordinary Jobs for

CREATIVE PEOPLE

Also in the Extraordinary Jobs series:

Extraordinary Jobs for

CREATIVE PEOPLE

ALECIA T. DEVANTIER & CAROL A. TURKINGTON

Ferguson
An imprint of Infobase Publishing

Extraordinary Jobs for Creative People

Ferguson
An imprint of Infobase Publishing
132 West 31st Street
New York NY 10001

Library of Congress Cataloging-in-Publication Data

Devantier, Alecia T.
  Extraordinary jobs for creative people / Alecia T. Devantier and Carol A. Turkington.
    p. cm.
  Includes bibliographical references and index.
  ISBN 0-8160-5853-9 (hc : alk. paper)
  1. Vocational guidance—United States. 2. Job descriptions. 3. Professions. 4. Creative ability.
I. Turkington, Carol. II. Title.
  HF5382.5.U5D425 2006
331.702'0973—dc22   2005019879

Ferguson books are available at special discounts when purchased in bulk quantities for businesses, associations, institutions, or sales promotions. Please call our Special Sales Department in New York at (212) 967-8800 or (800) 322-8755.

You can find Ferguson on the World Wide Web at http://www.fergpubco.com

Text design by Mary Susan Ryan-Flynn
Cover design by Salvatore Luongo

Printed in the United States of America

VB FOF 10 9 8 7 6 5 4 3 2 1

This book is printed on acid-free paper.

CONTENTS

ACKNOWLEDGMENTS

Thanks to all the people who helped with interviews and information, including Susan Shelly McGovern, Sandra Gurvis, Matt Kiernan, Mitch Bloom, Jill Arnold, Norm Arnold, Vicki Blizzard, Barbara Turkington, Judy Bednarz, Rich Donaldson, L.L. Bean, Madame Tussaud's, and Hallmark.

Thanks also to our editors James Chambers and Sarah Fogarty, to Vanessa Nittoli, to our agents Gene Brissie and Ed Claflin of Ed Claflin Literary Associates, and to Michael and Kara.

ARE YOU CUT OUT FOR A CREATIVE CAREER?

You tumble out of bed at 6:30 a.m., grab a suit from your closet, and jump in your Honda for a stop-and-go commute to your office, where you shuffle off to your desk for eight hours. If you're lucky, you get a window, and if you're really lucky, if you crane your neck you might catch a glimpse of the bay.

Are your toes curling up at the thought? Would you rather play with an Etch-a-Sketch than an electrocardiogram? Would you rather use your hands to sculpt a presidential candidate out of butter than stitch somebody's gashed cheek? Do you dream of creating something magnificent out of nothing, or are you solely focused on churning out that year-end report so you get your Christmas bonus?

Let's face it—some folks are made for creative endeavors, and they'll never fit inside a normal 9 to 5 time slot. And that's okay.

Do you dream of crafting a violin, building a sand sculpture, restoring a painting, or scribbling a bumper sticker slogan? Take some time to think about the kind of person you are, and the sorts of experiences you dream of having. Ask yourself: *Am I passionate about something?*

If you want a creative career, you'd better be, because many artistic careers don't pay that much. What those jobs do offer, however, is something much harder to measure—and that's a job that lets your spirit soar, that allows you to do what you love to do. You can't put a price on that.

Of course, loving what you do is only part of having a successful creative career. You've also got to be good at what you want to do. Most creative jobs require real talent, and if you're going to go after one of them, you need to be really good at it. Whether you're thinking of becoming an animator or a costume designer, you need to have the talent to do that job better than most other people.

You've got to be willing to work hard. "Too many times, kids have the idea that they'll graduate from art school and the world is just waiting for them," says caricature expert Keelan Parham. "Every school in the country has one kid who's a stand-out artist. But there are a lot of schools in the country," Parham says. "Talent is a gift from God. But the world isn't waiting for you to graduate from art school. If you expect the world to beat a path to your door to buy your art, then you're going to be a starving artist. You've got to work hard and treat your art like a real job. There's a lot of opportunity out here for young artists, no matter what the field. You've got to have a good work ethic to succeed."

It may not always be easy. Can you imagine what Michelangelo's mom said when he told her he wanted to paint church ceilings for a living? Have you inherited a lot of *shoulds* in thinking about the kind of person you want to be? These *shoulds* inside your head can be a major stumbling block in finding and enjoying a creative career. Perhaps the problem is financial—many of the finest art schools in this country are quite expensive.

As studio artist Nicholas Carbonaro explains, "you owe it to yourself to go to a good school. Don't cheat yourself if you want to be an artist. If you don't do what you were born to do—well, you're going to get older anyway. You might as well get older doing what you love to do. What you need to do."

You'll also need to realize that there also may be other people who aren't so happy with your career choice. You may hear complaints from your family and friends who just can't understand why you don't want a "regular" job. Some folks think art only qualifies as a hobby—surely you don't intend to make a living at it! If you confide your creative career dreams to some of these people, you may find they try to discourage you. Can you handle their continual skepticism?

Most people who enjoy creative jobs have gotten there by a circuitous route. If you decide to seek out a creative career, you'll almost certainly encounter setbacks. How do you handle adversity? How do you feel when you fail? If you can pick yourself up and keep going, you've probably got the temperament to survive the rocky road to a creative career.

At the same time, a creative career is usually more than a job—it's a way of looking at life. It's about learning to look at the world through curious eyes—to satisfy that irrepressible urge to create. Creative people often seem to see, hear, taste, and smell more intensely than everybody else. Being more aware of their surroundings, they are more involved in and aware of life.

Opportunities for creative jobs—especially in the arts—are expected to show an average growth of about 20 percent through 2012, according to the Bureau of Labor Statistics. Expanding electronic media and entertainment industries will offer opportunities for animators, illustrators, and graphic artists, but in general, competition for creative jobs will be keen. Opportunities for designers will grow at a faster-than-average rate of about 21 percent through 2012; job growth in this highly competitive area stems from increased demand for newer, high-tech industrial products as well as for Internet and video images.

Opportunities for museum-related creative types should grow at an average rate as well. Employment gains from organizations and the public's interest in historical information are nevertheless subject to funding cuts, which could limit opportunities. Competition is expected to be keen, but job applicants who have extensive computer skills should have the best opportunities.

AD AGENCIES

So if you're not self-employed, who hires creative types? Ad agencies almost always have art departments, because of their enormous flow of work. The agency staff includes art directors (in the larger agencies, creative directors supervise the work of art directors), layout artists, pasteup artists, graphic designers, and perhaps photo retouchers. Illustration and photography assignments are usually sent to freelancers or studios. Ad agencies can be exciting, creative places to work, and salaries are often higher than in any other category, since the creativity of the artist is of central importance to the success of the agency's work. Although starting salaries may be about the same as most other jobs just out of college, they tend to increase more quickly, especially in larger cities.

Advertising agencies are found in almost every town and city, but are clustered in the greatest numbers in New York, Chicago, and Los Angeles.

A special talent for originating verbal and visual messages plus a keen sense of marketing are essential if you are thinking about making a career in some aspect of advertising. You should be able to work well with a group of creative people, sometimes under the pressure of deadlines or during irregular hours, and enjoy the bustle and excitement typical of agency work.

STUDIO ART

A studio can become a substantial corporation, especially if the founder has a flair for leadership, but typically art studios are modest operations—and a terrific place for a beginning artist to start a creative career.

A *service studio* usually specializes in handling assignments from advertising agencies, and the pace tends to be rapid and exciting. *Design studios* may specialize in packaging or display, or industrial, interior, or textile design, or a specific type of art, such as pottery, glassblowing, or woodcarving. Some artists in design studios work as consultants. You can locate design studios in all larger cities, and in many smaller cities as well. Service studios tend to cluster in the larger urban centers, where advertising agencies are located. Almost any type of artist can find a job at a studio, which can be a great place for freelance artists to work.

NEWSPAPERS, MAGAZINES, AND BOOKS

If you're just starting out in a creative career, you might consider landing a job in an art department at a newspaper, magazine, or book publisher. Salaries here are decidedly lower than comparable work in agencies or studios, but because many publishing houses are large corporations, you'll be able to enjoy other benefits, such as retirement funds and paid vacations.

One advantage of publication work is that you can find a job almost anywhere; almost every town has a newspaper that hires one or two artists. Book and magazine publishers cluster in the larger cities, although there has been a recent trend toward locating headquarters in suburban areas. And if flexibility is your mantra, you can find lots of work as a freelance artist for most publications. You won't have the benefits of being a full-time employee, but if your creative spirit prefers to set your own hours and take on only the work you're interested in, this could be a fulfilling niche for you.

CORPORATE WORK

Some companies and manufacturers have their own art departments as a way of saving the cost of giving all their work to an outside organization. Every large company has a constant need for booklets, catalogs, sales presentations, reports, newsletters, and other promotional material. Advertising is generally handled by an ad agency because of the special nature of this work, but it's almost always less expensive for a company to produce non-advertising material in its own art department. Artists, art directors, designers, pasteup artists, writers, and occasionally photographers and illustrators are all hired by company art departments.

Company art departments usually offer a certain amount of job security with more benefits, such as health plans, retirement funds, and regular promotion. However, except for special training programs for minority groups or college study apprenticeships, the corporate art department typically prefers to hire experienced artists rather than beginners when an opening is available.

In addition, keep in mind that corporate art departments (with some exceptions) are often conservative in their design work.

STORES

Every large store or chain of stores must have an art department because of the high volume of daily newspaper advertising required. New shipments, and the rapid turnover of merchandise, make the retail advertising department a busy place. Stores may hire art directors, layout artists, display artists, pasteup artists, and fashion, furniture, and accessories illustrators. In addition, a large store typically keeps lots of freelance illustrators busy. Smaller stores may only need an art director operating as a one-man department hiring freelance artists when necessary. Store advertising departments often offer benefits such as retirement plans and special discounts on merchandise, and there's usually a chance to earn overtime during busy holiday seasons. Retailing is a volatile field with an exciting, sometimes hectic pace of work, and irregular hours may be common.

OTHER OPPORTUNITIES

In addition to those described above, there are lots of other opportunities for creative types you may not have thought about:

* architectural and interior design firms
* art galleries
* associations and clubs
* audiovisual production services
* box and carton manufacturers
* business forms services
* calendar and novelty manufacturers
* chambers of commerce
* clip art services
* clothing manufacturers
* college public relations offices
* fund-raising organizations
* greeting card companies
* hotel and motel headquarters
* Internet companies
* museums
* music publishers and record companies
* pottery and chinaware manufacturers
* sign studios
* theatrical and entertainment producers
* tour producers and agents
* toy and game manufacturers

A creative life isn't necessarily an easy one. You'll work hard—very hard. But if you allow yourself to explore the creative options in the world, you'll find that work and play become the same thing. Push past your doubts and fears, and let your journey to creativity begin!

Carol A. Turkington
Alecia T. Devantier

HOW TO USE THIS BOOK

Students face lots of pressure to decide what they want to be when they grow up. If you're not interested in a traditional 9 to 5 job and you're a creative spirit looking for a unique way to make a living, where can you go to find the answers to questions you might have about these exciting, creative, nontraditional jobs?

Where can you go to find out how to become a bead artist, creating art out of molten glass? Where do you learn how to be a gravestone carver? Is it really possible to make a living as a wax sculptor? Where would you go for training if you wanted to be a balloon artist or a sand sculptor? What's the job outlook for a video game designer?

Look no further! This book will take you inside the world of a number of different highly creative jobs, answering questions you might have, letting you know what to expect if you pursue that career, introducing you to someone making a living that way, and providing resources if you want to do further research.

THE JOB PROFILES

All job profiles in this book have been broken down into the following fact-filled sections: At a Glance, Overview, and Interview. Each offers a distinct perspective on the job, and taken together give you a full view of the job in question.

At a Glance

Each entry starts out with an At a Glance box, offering a snapshot of important basic information to give you a quick glimpse of that particular job, including salary, education/experience, personal attributes, requirements, and outlook.

✅ *Salary range.* What can you expect to make? Salary ranges for the jobs in this book are as accurate as possible; many are based on data from the U.S. Bureau of Labor Statistics' *Occupational Outlook Handbook*. Information also comes from individuals, actual job ads, employers, and experts in the field. It's important to remember that salaries for any particular job vary greatly depending on experience, geographic location, and level of education. For example, a small art gallery in a little Midwestern town would probably not pay someone as much as a larger international gallery in Manhattan.

✅ *Education/Experience.* What kind of education and experience does the job require? This section will give you some information about the types of education or experience requirements the job might have.

✅ *Personal attributes.* Do you have what it takes to do this job? How do you think of yourself? How would someone else describe you? This section will give you an idea of some of the personal characteristics and traits that might be useful in this career. These attributes were collected from articles written about the job, as well as recommendations from employers and people actually doing the jobs, working in the field.

✅ *Requirements.* Are you qualified? Some jobs have strict age or education requirements. You might as well make sure you meet any requirements before going any further with your job pursuit.

✓ *Outlook.* What are your chances of finding a job? This section is based in part on the *Occupational Outlook Handbook*, as well as interviews with employers and experts doing the jobs. This information is typically a "best guess" based on the information that is available right now, including changes in the economy, situations in the country and around the world, job trends and retirement levels, as well as many other factors that can influence the availability of jobs.

Overview

This section will give you an idea of what to expect from the job. For most of these jobs, there really is no such thing as an average day. Each new day, new job, or new assignment is a whole new creative adventure, bringing with it a unique set of challenges and rewards. This section provides a general overview of what a person holding this position might expect on a day-to-day basis.

This section also gives more details about how to get into the profession. It takes a more detailed look at the required training or education, if needed, giving an in-depth look at what to expect during that training or educational period. If there are no training or education requirements for the job, this section will provide some suggestions for getting the experience you'll need to be successful.

No job is perfect, and **Pitfalls** takes a look at some of the obvious and not-so-obvious pitfalls of the job. Don't let the pitfalls discourage you from pursuing the career; they are just things to be aware of while making your decision.

For many people, loving their job so much that they look forward to going to work every day is enough of a perk. **Perks** looks at some of the other perks of the job you may not have considered.

So what can you do *now* to start working toward the career of your dreams? **Get a Jump on the Job** will give you some ideas and suggestions for things that you can do now, even before graduating, to start preparing for this job. Opportunities include training programs, groups and organizations to join, as well as practical skills to learn.

Interview

In addition to taking a general look at the job, each entry features a discussion with someone who is lucky enough to do this job for a living. In addition to giving you an inside look at the job, the experts offer advice for people wanting to follow in their footsteps, pursuing a career in the same field.

APPENDIXES

Appendix A (Associations, Organizations, and Web Sites) lists places to look for additional information about each specific job, including professional associations, societies, unions, government organizations, Web sites, and periodicals. Associations and other groups are a great source of information, and there's an association for just about every job you can imagine. Many groups and associations have a student membership level, which you can join by paying a small fee. There are many advantages to joining an association, including the chance to make important contacts, receive helpful newsletters, and attend workshops or conferences. Some associations also offer scholarships that will make it easier to further your education. Other sources listed in this section include information about accredited training programs, forums, official government links, and more.

In **Appendix B (Online Career Resources)**, we've gathered some of the best general Web sites about unusual jobs in the creative area. Use these as a springboard to your own Internet research. All of this information was current as this book was written, but Web site addresses do change. If you can't find what you're looking for at a given address, do a simple Web search.

The page may have been moved to a different location.

In Appendix C (Art Schools) we've listed art schools by state.

READ MORE ABOUT IT

In this back-of-the-book listing, we've gathered some helpful books that can give you more detailed information about each job we discuss in this book. Find these at the library or bookstore if you want to learn even more about creative jobs.

ANIMATOR

OVERVIEW

Shrek rescues Princess Fiona from the jaws of the dragon. Nemo is stolen from his coral reef home. Mike jumps through closets to harness the screams of children. All of these events come to life through the work of animators, whose job it is to bring the inanimate world to life.

Exactly how it's brought to life can be done any number of different ways. You can draw it, make a model of it and move it, put it on a computer, or you can cut out bits of paper and move them around. You can even move whole people around, photographing them one frame at a time, so they can move without walking. All of these are different forms of animation.

Most animation jobs are in cartoons or commercials (of which more than 20 percent have animated sequences).

In drawn animation—also known as traditional animation or cell animation—you draw pictures and photograph them sequentially in order to make them appear to move when projected one after another. These sequential drawings are the roots of animation, which is why animators should have strong artistic inclinations. Most are computer or technical animators, whose jobs require less graphic design expertise but more familiarity with animation programs such as Macromedia Director. Nearly all animators work as part of a team and have a specific area of specialization.

Back when pencil-and-paper animation was the standard, animators could only work in two dimensions (2-D).

AT A GLANCE

Salary Range

From less than $25,830 to more than $85,160, with an average of $43,980. Average annual earnings for animators in the motion picture and video industries are slightly higher, at about $58,840.

Education/Experience

A bachelor of fine arts (BFA) or master of fine arts (MFA) degree can be helpful, although it is not typically required. Computer experience is often important. The minimum requirement is a high school diploma or GED plus experience.

Personal Attributes

Broad artistic and technical skills. Communication skills and the ability to collaborate, plus a good sense of color, motion, and form. The work requires long hours, self-discipline, patience, and the ability to work with others.

Requirements

Excellent drawing and computer skills. Computer science or computer engineering certificates are needed to work in computer animation. Knowledge of and training in computer graphics and other visual display software are critical elements of many jobs in these fields.

Outlook

Growth in motion picture and video industries will provide new job opportunities for animators, but competition for most jobs is keen because opportunities are relatively few, and there are usually lots more people interested in these positions than there are openings. However, if you are talented and are able to get your work viewed, you stand a reasonable chance of finding a job.

Now, with high-tech computer software, animators can create three-dimensional (3-D) animation, giving characters and scenes depth as well as height and width. Already, most animators work with computers, using pencil-like instruments to point, draw, and create on their computer screens.

If you dream of bringing Spiderman and Batwoman to life, your best bet is to hone your strong art skills and spend some time getting familiar with computers. You can go to a school to learn the animation trade, but many animators who started out working with pencils and paper have taught themselves to use new computer animation software to increase their efficiency. While the first programs weren't really easy to use, newer animation software is a snap to master. As in most fine arts fields, no formal education or training is required, but it is extremely difficult to achieve the level of professionalism expected in this industry without formal study. A bachelor's or graduate degree in graphic design with an emphasis on computer skills is really helpful in getting interviews.

Certain universities offer specific one-semester courses in computer animation on Oxberry Animation Cameras (the kind that filmed *Fantasia*), or using Silicon Graphics computer work stations with 2- and 3-D software (the kind used in *Jurassic Park* and *The Mask*).

If you dream of bringing art to life, you can find work as an animator in feature films, television, in advertising, on the Internet, in CD-ROM or video production, product design, architecture, or interior design. Animators draw by hand and use computers to create the large series of pictures that form the animated images or special effects seen in movies, television programs, and computer games.

Some animators draw storyboards for TV commercials, movies, and animated features. Storyboards present a series of scenes similar to a comic strip and allow the directors, producers, or executives to evaluate proposed creative media. Storyboards also serve as guides for arranging actors and cameras on the TV or movie set and to other details that need to be taken care of during production.

When it comes to finding a job, the art director or client will look at evidence of your talent and skill by reviewing your artist's portfolio—a collection of hand-made, computer-generated, photographic, or printed samples of your best work. Assembling a successful portfolio requires skills usually developed in a bachelor's degree program or through other training in art or visual communications.

If you're hoping to get hired by a major animation studio, be prepared to show them a videotape of your animation. They'll be looking for great potential in animation, lighting, modeling, or writing.

Many people spend their own money (between $5,000 and $125,000) producing short, animated movies to showcase their talents, and then enter these in animation competitions for the exposure and financial reward.

There are different ways that you can get started in the field of animation. Here are a few types of jobs that animators do:

* **Inbetweener:** Most artists enter the world of animation by starting as inbetweeners—the artists who help the animators and animation assistants complete the action of a scene. An *inbetween* is one of the transition drawings between two extreme drawings—the key drawings that distill the essence of an animated action. The inbetweens fill in the action between these key drawings. If you

Steve Silver, animator

London-born animator Stephen Silver, creator of Disney's Kim Possible, wanted to be a professional artist for just about his entire life. He first got involved in drawing at the age of six when he found an artist's original sketchbook lying in his backyard. From that point on, he knew that drawing would be his purpose in life.

In 1992, Silver got his professional start drawing caricatures at amusement parks, eventually moving on to establish his own illustration business and caricature concession company called Silvertoons. Four years later, he was hired as a graphic designer for the clothing company "No Fear," and then in 1997, he was hired at Warner Bros. Television Animation as a character designer. He's been working in the animation industry ever since.

"I enjoy the art of character design so much that I've gone on to teach the art form part time," he explains. "I believe there are three treasures to success in life: determination, passion, and desire. These are the three rules I live by, giving me what it takes to keep on drawing. I hope my artwork inspires you, like so many other artists works have inspired me."

Today he works as head character designer for Disney Television Animation, for whom he created Kim Possible; he's also developed Danny Phantom/Crash Nebula for Nickelodeon Television Animation. He teaches character design for the Animation Academy, and also worked on Dragon Tales for Columbia Tristar Television Animation.

Winner of the 2001 Caricaturist of the Year from the National Caricaturist Network, Silver is largely self-taught. "Art is hard work, but it's also fun. It's about thinking, planning, creative problem solving, and most of all, determination."

begin as an inbetweener, you'll usually work in a team and learn to imitate the animator's drawings and line quality.

* **Layout artist:** The layout artist creates the foundation for the animation by rendering background layouts for each scene, usually referring to storyboards and other research materials. These layouts don't appear in the final production, but they're critical for the positioning and perspective of the animation. Layouts are usually done with graphite pencil on punched animation paper in order to provide a stage in which the animators will animate their characters and effects. Layout artists also prepare a blueprint (or underdrawing) to be rendered in color by the background painters.

* **Storyboard artist:** Some animators begin as storyboard artists, who create storyboards by interpreting, planning shots, visualizing the story before drawing it, and maintaining continuity among the shots. Of course, you shouldn't expect to graduate from school and start out as a storyboard artist—most begin as an assistant, where you'll be expected to do cleanup and revisions, eventually working up to preparing some parts of the storyboard under supervision. This work involves a lot of cutting and pasting, drawing

and quick sketching, perspective and composition, and—most important—story development and interpretation.

* **2-D animator:** If you want to become a 2-D animator, you'll need to develop your skills through life drawing, composition, and perspective courses, studying proportion, line of action, structure, and basic anatomy, while working in areas as varied as animation, character design, cleanup, modeling, and storyboarding. Although companies like Pixar have developed 3-D animation to a high art, 2-D animation continues to be a growing and popular medium, especially since classical 2-D skills are the foundation for most 3-D work.

* **3-D animator:** 3-D animators are concerned with many of the same things as their 2-D colleagues—you'll still need skills in life drawing, concept drawing, composition, character design, and so on. As a 3-D animator, however, you'll also deal more extensively with modeling, texturing, and lighting, using software tools and packages such as PhotoShop, SoftImage, Alias/Wavefront, Maya, and others.

Pitfalls

The job market can be tight, and it can be hard to break into the business. The low wages and the struggle to emerge as a talented individual are difficult obstacles. For creative people, the push to produce work to someone else's specifications for their approval or disapproval can be frustrating. Expect to pay your dues at first by working as an intern, an assistant,

or an inbetweener before moving into the animation field.

Perks

For artistic souls, the job of animation is more like play than work. The act of creation can be a creatively fulfilling, exciting, and well-paid way to earn a living. Animation studios are typically places filled with interesting, unique, and creative people doing work they truly love.

Get a Jump on the Job

If you're interested in animation, you need to spend lots of time practicing drawing skills—and using a computer for more than just e-mail! Developing your artistic and technological skills is the best way to prepare for a career in animation. In choosing a school to learn animation, look for one that focuses on traditional skills, drawing, painting, sculpture, and cinematography. Ask the school how they will help you build an effective portfolio of your work—not just a collection of assignments, but a well-developed presentation of your unique style and technical skills. Ask the school how well their theater and film departments are integrated with their 2-D and 3-D art departments.

Look for a school that balances both electronic and traditional art, and avoid simply learning software packages that will be outdated in a year or two. (Many studios use proprietary software that you can't learn in school anyway.) Get enough computer skills to know you can learn more, but concentrate on the more expressive traditional skills. What really counts is your fundamental drawing skills and your willingness to learn the craft.

When it comes to learning the specifics of the trade, there's no substitute for an apprentice situation under a great animator in a studio setting. Draw as much as you can. Apply what you learn in life drawing to your cartoon drawing, try to be flexible about style, and study the animation of the past.

Many studios offer apprenticeships or internships. For example, Pixar offers paid technical internships throughout the year. Nontechnical internships are typically offered in the summer, depending on departmental needs. When internships are available, they are posted on the Pixar Web site: http://jobsearch.pixar.careers. monster.com. Only college students may apply.

ARCHITECTURAL ILLUSTRATOR

OVERVIEW

Do you ever look at buildings and wonder about the people who thought up their design? Do you like to draw house plans on paper? Artists who work closely with architects—but in a purely artistic way—are called *architectural illustrators*, and their job is to draw what a house looks like after its floor plan is drawn by the architect.

Architectural illustrators must have a keen understanding of architecture and building design, and be able to read blueprints and floor plans. A few architectural illustrators are on the staffs of large architectural firms, but most firms don't have a designated illustrator. There are a limited number of architectural illustration firms, but more than half of architectural illustrators are self-employed and work on a freelance basis.

Architectural illustration used to be done completely by hand, but computer programs such as Architectural Desktop, AutoCAD, and Viz Render are increasingly being used in illustration projects. However, some architectural illustrators still do pen-and-ink or watercolor drawings, and others combine computer-generated views and hand-drawn illustrations.

An architectural illustrator works with an architect or team of architects to create an illustration of an architectural plan. As an architectural illustrator, you'll create interior and exterior views. Three-dimensional illustrations are becoming increasingly popular because they allow customers to virtually walk through a

designed building, experiencing the space, layout, and lighting. Proponents of 3-D illustrating say it allows buyers to more effectively see the project before it's built, giving them a head start on design and decorating options.

Architectural illustrators are important to architectural projects. While architecture contains elements of both art and science, many architects tend to stay more to the science side. Their clients, however, want to be able to see what the building will look like when it's finished, something that's difficult to do from looking at blueprints. Architects depend

Robert Becker, architectural illustrator

Robert Becker decided halfway through his second year in architectural school that he was going to be an architectural illustrator. That made it easy for him to focus his studies on art, while taking architectural courses as electives. As a result, he graduated from college as an art major, with a minor in architecture. That path, however, isn't typical. Most architectural illustrators are trained as architects, and are actually working as architects when they make the move to illustrator, Becker says.

"I'm sure that there are some people who get into the field purely from an artistic avenue, but I think that's rare," Becker says. "Every top architectural illustrator I can think of started as an architect."

Becker was happy to discover early on that his goal was architectural illustration instead of architecture. "I'm so glad that I found that out when I did," he says. "That let me bail out of everything but the architectural design courses and concentrate on art. I took a lot of architectural courses as electives, but I could pick and choose. I didn't need to know how a building stands."

Once he was out of school, Becker got a job in New York City with an architectural illustration firm, but he also did freelance work on the side. Freelance work is important, he says, because it allows more people to see your work, in addition to providing extra money.

Working with other illustrators turned out to very valuable for Becker.

"Everything I learned about what I do on a daily basis, I learned from other illustrators," Becker says. "Actually, I learned from their mistakes. It was easier for me to see their mistakes than it was for them, and then I'd remember what worked and what didn't work."

While many architectural illustrators are moving toward computer-generated illustrations, Becker still works entirely by hand, primarily with watercolors. "Some of the computer stuff is really great," Becker says. "But I do all my work by hand. It's not that I don't see the value of the computer, but when you use it, you have to be willing to take what it spits out. I'm not willing to do that."

Often, he says, it takes less time for him to do a watercolor illustration than it does for an illustrator to generate a computer image of a plan. He has been working entirely on a freelance basis since 1995. While he does most of his work in his studio in Orinda, California, he's happy to work in his clients' offices so they can see the illustrations in progress.

"They can watch me work—look over my shoulder and make suggestions," Becker says. "A lot of illustrators wouldn't do that, but it works for me."

The most important ability for an architectural illustrator, he says, is to be able to quickly understand a client's vision, and to be able to express the vision of the client—not your own vision— on paper. "Some illustrators want the design to be theirs," he says. "But I let my ego out of it. I want to get what's in my client's head out on the piece of paper."

Becker's advice for anyone considering a career as an architectural illustrator is to get the education and training you need, and to learn how to market yourself and your work. Join an organization such as the American Society of Architectural Illustrators and get to know other people in the field. It's also important to develop skills that will allow you to run your own business, and to know the value of your work.

"Artists notoriously never think their work is good enough or worth very much," Becker says. "You can't be afraid to charge what you're worth. Your clients have to be willing to pay for your work."

on architectural illustrators to provide top quality illustrations of the finished project—before the project has started—and value illustrators who can quickly provide them with accurate, attractive work.

Pitfalls

The art and science of architectural illustration are changing quickly, and you might need to participate in ongoing education in order to keep up. Most illustrating jobs are located around metropolitan areas, which could be a disadvantage if you don't want to live in or near a city.

Perks

Once you've gotten some experience as an architectural illustrator and made some contacts, you could start your own business. A good architectural illustrator generally does not have trouble finding jobs, and your salary can increase quickly once you've established yourself in the field.

Get a Jump on the Job

Explore the software used in architectural illustrating, or buy an architectural drawing/construction kit available through lots of catalogs. Take some basic drawing classes or look for art lessons on architectural drawing online or in books.

ART CONSERVATOR

OVERVIEW

Art conservators look like the magicians of the art world, taking a damaged piece of art and bringing it back to its original glory. They are actually trained art historians, chemists, and materials scientists with the manual dexterity and color sense of skilled artists. Good conservators must be as talented as the original artist so that their handiwork doesn't leap out as a clumsy repainting of the original art.

If you dream of creating your own *David* or *Last Supper*, a career in art conservation isn't for you. Conservation has been called "the humble art" exactly because the job is all about preserving the past, not creating something new. Conservators manage, care for, preserve, and document works of art, artifacts, and specimens created by others, which may require substantial historical, scientific, and archeological research.

Using X rays, chemical testing, microscopes, special lights, and other laboratory equipment and techniques, conservators examine objects and determine their condition, their need for treatment or restoration, and the appropriate method for preserving them. They document their findings and treat items to minimize their deterioration or to restore them to their original state. Conservators usually specialize in a particular material or group of objects, such as documents and books, paintings, decorative arts, textiles, metals, or architectural material.

AT A GLANCE

Salary Range

$16,000 to $200,000 and up, depending on experience and place of employment; average is between $40,000 and $60,000.

Education/Experience

Usually requires a master's degree in conservation or a closely related field, together with substantial experience.

Personal Attributes

Attention to detail, meticulous work habits, interest in art, fine hand-eye coordination.

Requirements

Degree in art-related field with lots of chemistry.

Outlook

The job outlook is fair, particularly for graduates of conservation programs, but competition is stiff for the limited number of openings in these programs, and applicants need a technical background. Students who successfully complete a conservation program, have knowledge of a foreign language, and are willing to relocate will have an advantage over less qualified candidates.

For example, if you specialized in painting, you'd preserve and restore damaged and faded paintings, applying solvents and cleaning agents to clean the surfaces, reconstructing or retouching damaged areas, and applying preservatives to protect the paintings. As you can imagine, this is highly detailed work reserved for experts in the field.

Conservators may work under contract to treat particular items, rather than as regular employees of a museum or other institution. They may work as freelancers or as employees of conservation laboratories or regional conservation centers that contract with museums. Some large museums employ their own stable of conservators.

Art conservators apply science to the technical study, preservation, and treatment of art objects. A professional art conservator can advise clients on how to display, store, and preserve special objects and how to preserve public art and historic buildings and sites. They can advise clients on disaster planning for areas prone to earthquakes, fires, or floods and give advice about treating surfaces of an object flaking, fading, or discoloring. Among the most significant and controversial recent efforts of art conservation have been the cleaning of Michelangelo's fresco on the Sistine Chapel ceiling and of his marble sculptures, and similar work on art by da Vinci and other Renaissance artists.

Conservation professionals combine unique skills in the arts and sciences gained through study and training in art history, chemistry, studio art, and related disciplines. They are experts in the conservation of paintings, paper, books, photographs, textiles, decorative arts, sculpture, and wooden artifacts as well as architectural, archeological, natural science, and ethnographic materials.

Conservators are concerned with a number of factors in preserving an object, including determining structural stability, counteracting chemical and physical deterioration, and performing conservation treatment based on an evaluation of the aesthetic, historic, and scientific characteristics of the object. They have lots of practical experience and a broad range of theoretical and scientific knowledge.

Sometimes people get confused about the difference between *restoration* and *conservation*. Restoration refers to the reconstruction of the aesthetic appearance of an object. Although restoration can be one aspect of conservation, conservation involves examination, scientific analysis, and research to determine original structure, materials, and extent of loss. Conservators also treat the object's structure and environment to slow down future deterioration.

As a conservator, you'll examine the object first before suggesting a treatment, and then give your client a written preliminary report with a description of the proposed treatment, expected results, and estimated cost. You'll also need to provide a treatment report afterward, listing materials and procedures used, plus a set of before and after photos. Recommendations for continued care and maintenance may also be provided.

There are two ways to become an art conservator. You can begin an extended apprenticeship with an established, respected conservator for five to seven years, or you could attend one of the five university art conservation graduate programs in North America. This is not so easy, since each program only accepts four to ten students a year. If you're interested in a graduate program, you'll need a considerable amount of undergraduate credits in chemistry and physics, art history, and studio art. The graduate programs also require that a student have one to three years of experience in an established art conservation laboratory.

Most graduate programs are three years long: two years in school and a year of an internship in a museum, regional laboratory, or with a conservator in private practice. After graduation, students will spend one to four years in fellowship positions, usually in large museum conservation laboratories. The most important qualification in paintings conservation is experience. Essential, too, is continuing education in the field. Conservators often attend national and international workshops, symposiums, congresses, and conferences.

So what exactly does a conservator do? Let's say your aunt has an old painting that has yellowed and faded over time, so that the background has lost its true color. If you were a conservator working on this painting, you'd first examine it, identifying the artist. Trained as an art historian, you should be aware of the style of that period, the painting technique, and the materials available to an artist of that time. This will help you identify the pigments and fabrics that were popular and available to the artist and help you determine the best approach for the restoration.

You might remove the frame and look under the thin area hidden beneath the edge of the frame (called the *tacking edge*) to uncover pigments that are light and clear, which can help you see what the true colors should be. If your solvent tests suggest that dirt can be safely removed, you'd take a cotton swab and carefully clean away the surface dirt, while avoiding the layers of paint underneath.

If you discover a layer of varnish, you can perform a small cleaning test to remove it. Wearing a jeweler's head-mounted visor, you can carefully remove each layer of varnish and then wash the area with a retarding solvent to remove any leftover solvent to reveal the underlying image. No pigment is removed in this process. This is delicate work that must progress quite slowly, with each stroke viewed under a magnifying lens.

This meticulous chemical process must be performed by a person with a trained and steady hand and an educated, experienced eye. A conservator must make sure that the solvent doesn't go too far, either removing the original pigment or chemically burning the surface. There's no margin for error since any loss of pigment is irrevocable.

Conservators continue this complicated process, examining with a magnifying glass and a microscope, using different lights, making notes and taking photographs at each stage to carefully document every part of the restoration, until all the old varnish is removed.

A conservator, trained in material science, also can fix any rips or tears in the painting itself. Conservators will often remove the painting from its stretcher and cover the front with a protective facing composed of wet paper and emulsion. This protects the surface while he or she uses a surgeon's scalpel to carefully remove years of dirt and grime from the back of the canvas. Any material used to repair or strengthen the canvas must be able to be removed without harming or discoloring the original paint.

Finally, a conservator will remove residual adhesive and restretch the painting onto a new museum-quality stretcher. Once this is complete, the conservator is ready to repaint.

The conservator—a trained artist—next brushes a synthetic, nonyellowing, removable varnish over the face of the painting. This is called an *isolating varnish*, because it separates the original painting from any paint that will be added to reconstruct the design. Dry pigments are used in a synthetic, nonyellowing medium in areas of color loss, using exactly the same colors, texture and surface sheen of the surrounding areas. The conservator's paint should only touch areas of actual paint

Katrina de Carbonel, painting/textile conservator

Katrina de Carbonel of Rowayton, Connecticut, started out as a fine arts major in college, until reality struck: 99 percent of fine artists she knew couldn't earn a living at their craft once they graduated. After volunteering at an art museum in Los Angeles, she learned more about art conservation and realized this could be a way to combine her love of art with a viable career. She decided to apply for graduate study at Harvard.

"Art conservation is an extremely competitive field," she says. "There were 80 applications for two places at Harvard when I was going to school." After earning a graduate degree in art conservation from Harvard, de Carbonel wrote to the Louvre and landed a job in Paris. Since then, she has worked on French historic monuments, in museums all over Europe, and for a variety of museums in Washington, D.C., including the Corcoran Museum of Art, the National Gallery of Art, and the Textile Museum. She has also worked for several private museums, such as the Armand Hammer Museum and the J. Paul Getty Museum.

Her work as a freelance conservationist enabled her to work from home and raise her children.

The work of a conservationist is always different, and that's also part of the appeal, de Carbonel says. "Techniques change for each piece," she says. "You have to vary the way you work on something. It's an opportunity to learn."

Although she's willing to work on any type of painting, she prefers working on old pieces. "You have to be passionate about what you're doing," she says. "And you have to be extremely patient."

"Art conservationists don't make large fortunes at this work," she warns budding conservators. "We do it out of love. It's so satisfying. It's like curing people without any blood. Most of the time, the clients are delighted with your work."

loss and should never overlap undamaged original paint. Once this painting is finished, the conservator brushes on one final coat of protective varnish.

The restoration process can take anywhere from a few days to more than a year, depending on the size and complexity of the work. All materials used in the restoration are noninvasive and can easily be removed without endangering paint layers or affecting the work in any way.

Pitfalls

Jobs in art conservation are hard to find and the training is long and arduous. Considering the amount of education and skill that is required, the field is not particularly well paid.

Perks

Those who love art, art history, and fine things can find glory in spending their life immersed in the preservation and conservation of artwork. There is quite a lot of glamour associated with this job, and highly trained conservators can find work in top museums all over the world.

Get a Jump on the Job

There are three primary colleges that offer programs in art conservation in the United States: Buffalo State University, New York University, and the University of Delaware. Because there are only a few graduate programs in museum conservation techniques in the United States, competition for entry to these programs is keen. You can prepare by taking lots of chemistry, archeology or studio art, and art history, as well as getting some work experience. For some programs, knowledge of a foreign language is also helpful.

Conservation apprenticeships or internships as an undergraduate can help win you a spot in graduate school, which lasts two to four years (the latter years include internship training).

It's also possible to enter the field via apprenticeships with museums, nonprofit organizations, and conservators in private practice. However, you should supplement your apprenticeship with courses in chemistry, studio art, and history. Apprenticeship training, although acceptable, is usually a more difficult route into the conservation profession.

ART DEALER

OVERVIEW

It sounds like a glamorous profession—and it is. Art dealers sell artwork that they've found and bought, reselling at a profit. Having many clients who want to buy art is critical for success in this field, so it's important to be able to maintain contact with lots of artists and wholesalers willing to sell their works to dealers at a discounted price for resale.

Art dealers must be aware of general trends in the market in order to know what to buy for their target markets. The top dealers can predict changes in the tastes of their current and potential clients.

Ultimately, dealers hope to work for collectors willing to spend from $1 million to $12 million for a piece. As a result, dealers commonly search for extraordinary works of art for particular clients and help them develop their taste.

Although a degree in art history can't hurt, what's really important to success as an art dealer is being able to recognize quality, rarity, and value—and you can only recognize those if you have looked at a lot of things.

There are many paths to becoming an art dealer. Even if you've earned a Ph.D., you'll typically start out on the lowest rung of the artistic totem pole. Many dealers begin with degrees in art history and work their ways up as assistants in other galleries, developing the contacts with clients and artists to enable them to strike out on their own. Others are former museum and auction house curators who decide to establish galleries specializing in a particular area of art. A few artists

AT A GLANCE

Salary Range
$44,740 to $115,570.

Education/Experience
A college degree in art history is useful. Most art dealers begin by working as assistants to other art dealers or in museums.

Personal Attributes
Being a successful art dealer requires skills in finding and taking care of clients, as well as knowledge of salesmanship. Great communication and people skills, as well as a good eye for art and design, are essential.

Requirements
None.

Outlook
Fair. The world of art is competitive and volatile.

discover they have the business and social skills necessary to sell art, and they use their contacts with other artists to develop a body of work to represent.

As with any self-employment venture, strong business and sales skills are vital, since most money you'll earn is generated by personal sales pitches to prospective buyers. Access to lots of money can also help, since gallery cash flow comes in fits and starts. To survive in the long run, a dealer must be able to withstand dry spells; one way to do this is to join a partnership in which one partner contributes capital and the other contributes the connections and knowledge to successfully operate the business.

The very best dealers develop a reputation for anticipating changes in taste and value. Most dealers specialize in a period, style, or type of art, such as

Mark Gruber, art dealer

Mark Gruber was halfway through premed courses at Utica College in New York when he suddenly realized what he really loved was art—so he switched his major to theater and the arts. After graduation, he opened a framing business and then opened a larger gallery—the Mark Gruber Gallery—in New Paltz, New York.

"I was around artists all the time," he explained. "It was just a natural thing to fall into."

He represents a group of 15 artists and has produced a variety of shows and events at his gallery highlighting the work of more than 20—mostly Hudson Valley landscape painters. He chooses art to sell based on what works well in the space and seems to suit his clientele. His prices are usually established by the artist, although Gruber may suggest a price range he feels is reasonable. The works are then sold on commission.

He keeps current with the world of art by looking at works of art, reading trade magazines and local newspapers, and talking with his artist friends and associates.

Despite his love for New York art, it's not an easy job. "I always say there's only about 2 percent of the public that's buying art," he says, "and fine art, even less than that. It's definitely a hard road to go, but longevity does help me here."

seventeenth-century painting, textiles, or contemporary sculpture. All dealers must keep up with developments in the art world, particularly in their areas of specialty, so their careers depend upon maintaining a wide range of contacts among critics, curators, auction houses, artists, and collectors.

If you love the social whirl, this is the career for you, since much of the business is conducted at openings and in sales proposals made to collectors and museum curators. In fact, most successful art dealers enjoy spending time with people in the art world and cultivating contacts with people who are interested in art.

It's not an easy job, finding exceptional works of art for a gallery to acquire. Sellers don't usually walk in carrying top-quality art—it must be discovered. Dealers often read sale catalogs, talk to other galleries and museums, and attend auctions—always searching for unusual pieces, checking out families experiencing financial problems or a recent death.

The pleasures and possibilities for huge profits in the profession seem to offer rewards that balance the risks in art dealing, however. Many dealers have long and successful careers, and there is a steady supply of those whose taste and talent in the art world leads them to establish galleries.

Pitfalls

It can be difficult to maintain patience and develop the negotiation skills required to cope with the temperaments of the very rich. Others find the disparity in income to be disheartening; dealers may start at an annual salary of $30,000, plus commission. In addition, art markets are notoriously volatile, and the fortunes of gallery owners rise and fall with the markets.

Perks

People who become art dealers do so because they have a passion for art. The pleasure that comes with making a living combined with the freedom of owning one's own business can make this an extremely gratifying career. Those who love fine art and beautiful things can find great joy in living and working among exquisite art.

Get a Jump on the Job

If you love art, spend lots of your free time at art museums and reading about art history. Try visiting antique stores and chatting with owners who know a lot about art. Pick up as much information as you can, before going to college and majoring in art history.

BALLOON SCULPTURE ARTIST

OVERVIEW

When most people hear the term *balloon sculpture* or *balloon art*, they think of the infamous balloon dogs popularized by circus clowns and midway artists. But balloon dogs are just the tip of the iceberg when it comes to balloon art and sculpture—especially compared to something like an octopus with an arm span of 40 feet, standing 10 feet tall, created with hundreds or even thousands of balloons of all sizes and shapes and colors.

Many balloon artists are self-employed small business owners. Much of their work comes from creating balloon bouquets—a popular alternative to flowers for birthdays, anniversaries, and other special occasions. And because most balloon businesses also offer delivery, this lets the artist enjoy the recipient's reaction to the creation, depending on who does the delivering. Balloon businesses also create small arrangements for other events, such as table centerpieces for weddings, bar and bat mitzvahs, business meetings, conventions, fund-raising events, and parties. Depending on the needs of the customers, a balloon artist might be able to specialize in a particular area, such as balloons for weddings. Generally, however, balloon artists need to be flexible and create whatever type of bouquet or sculpture is needed to meet their customers' needs.

When hired to do a large project, balloon artists often find themselves creating an arch, column, or tree for an event, or maybe orchestrating a large balloon drop. Sometimes, balloon artists are asked to create huge sculptures for an event. Depending on the event, its organizers, and its budget, the only limitation might be the artist's imagination. The customer might come to the artist with an idea in mind, or simply a theme around which the sculpture should be created. Then it's up to the artist to figure how to use balloons to bring that idea or theme to life.

AT A GLANCE

Salary Range
An employee with a Certified Balloon Artist (CBA) credential can expect to earn $8 to $12 per hour; a self-employed CBA could make $25,000 to $125,000 a year or more.

Education/Experience
None required, but if you plan to open your own business, classes in management, accounting, marketing, and other business-related courses would be very helpful.

Personal Attributes
Self-motivated and detail-oriented, with a good feel for color and design, excellent fine motor skills, and the personality to market oneself as well as one's work.

Requirements
Must be able to work with latex-based products for long periods of time without allergic reaction.

Outlook
This industry is linked to the economy, but it is expected to continue to grow. People considering opening a balloon business need to keep in mind that it's very difficult to make a living on deliveries alone, and they'll need to do corporate or private events as well.

Cornelia Franklin, certified balloon artist

Back when stay-at-home mom Cornelia Franklin was making and selling personalized books at fairs and craft shows in 1989, the idea of becoming a balloon artist was the farthest thing from her mind. She was selling books through mail order and at educational conferences, eventually operating a pushcart at local shopping malls, where she used Mylar balloons to attract attention.

"People always wanted the balloons," she noticed. In fact, so popular were the balloons that she decided to check into selling those, too. One week after she started selling Mylar balloons, an ad agency asked her to decorate for a corporate event. "I realized that there was a huge market for balloons in general, and decorating too."

Still selling out of a pushcart and then moving to a kiosk, the business grew quickly. "It got out of control. The demand was high." Franklin took her husband to a weeklong International Balloon Arts Convention in San Francisco, and when they got home, he resigned his day job, cashed in his retirement, and together they opened their first store.

Proving that your past experiences and education can always be useful, Franklin's husband put his marketing degree to work, promoting the business and building a strong corporate client list. Not to be outdone, Franklin called upon her experience as a high school mascot. She ordered a hot pink gorilla costume that she saw in an industry magazine ad and used it to promote the business and make balloon deliveries. The gorilla costume proved so successful that they changed the name of the business to A Pink Gorilla.

To get the training necessary to become a successful balloon artist, Franklin recommends artists work for a company and then get certified. She's found that it takes about six months to master the skills, so don't give up; with time, patience, practice and determination, they will come. If you do want to open your own business, Franklin recommends taking as many business classes as you can in high school, or at a community college.

"It's a lot of work," she warns. "It's fun, but it's work! I love owning my own business and working with my husband. I have no problem getting up at 3:45 a.m. for a job if necessary. At the end of the day, I know we've made people happy, and that's an awesome thing."

She also believes, "If you put your mind to something, you can do anything. If you have the desire to do balloons, do it; jump in with two feet, and do it!"

To see some of Franklin's whimsical balloon bouquets and other spectacular creations, visit her Web site at http://www.apinkgorilla.com.

There are no educational requirements to become a balloon artist, but many individuals working in the field are certified balloon artists (CBAs). Becoming a CBA gives you more skills and accreditation, both of which are very important in the business world. To become a CBA, you must be 18 years old and work for or own a Qualatex Balloon Network (QBN) member business.

To become a CBA, you'll need to pass five written exams covering different areas of balloon arrangements, décor, and more. After passing the exams, you must submit photographs from four different classic balloon décor jobs; photos from balloon sculptures or centerpieces are not allowed. After meeting those requirements, you must pass the CBA four-hour practical exam where you demonstrate your skills and knowledge.

There are many ways you can learn the skills needed to become a successful balloon artist and a CBA. You can start with some of the many balloon books and videos on the market. Some titles to get you started are listed in Read More About It at the end of this book. Most of these titles focus on the art of balloon twisting, and while balloon twisting is not the focus of large balloon sculptures, many artists incorporate some twisting or twisting techniques in their sculptures. Doing some basic twisting and working with balloons will help to tune your fine motor skills, an important quality for balloon artists.

Of course, hands-on learning experience is probably best to master the skills and techniques. Classes and workshops are offered all around the country by various individuals and organizations. Another great way to learn is to work for a balloon sculptor. You might start out doing menial tasks, but the tips and tricks you learn from working with an artist will be invaluable to you as you advance in your career.

Perks

Every day is a new job and a new challenge, so there's no chance of getting bored. You have the opportunity to work with your clients planning fun and/or unique pieces for their events.

Pitfalls

Balloon sculpture is hard work and you don't get a lot of time off. You often have to work when others are off (for example, weekends and holidays). If you're a business owner, there will be times when money is tight, and there may even be some weeks that you don't get a paycheck because paying the bills and the salaries of other employees comes first.

Get a Jump on the Job

Practice, practice, practice! Balloons are inexpensive and readily available, so get an assortment of sizes, shapes, and colors, and start experimenting. Once you get going, you can create sculptures and arrangements to celebrate the birthdays of your family members and friends. As your skills improve, volunteer to do small-scale sculptures for local events like school fairs, fund-raisers, civic events, and festivals. Look for an opportunity to work at a balloon shop after school or during your summer vacation.

BOARD GAME DESIGNER

OVERVIEW

Whether you're a fan of old traditional games like *Monopoly* or *Clue!* or you're happier playing *Alien!* or *Rat-a-Tat-Cat*, board games never go out of fashion.

Every board game you've ever played has been created by a board game designer somewhere who planned every aspect of the game. A game design is considered successful when participants want to play it over and over again.

Board game designers generally fall into one of two patterns—there's the lone inventor who stumbles onto one great idea, or the prolific seasoned pros who can come up with one great idea after another. (It's the latter group who can really make a good living at game board designing.)

If you're interested in becoming a successful board game designer, you'll need to have a good sense of what makes an exciting game, and a good idea and instinct for how a particular game should be designed. In general, the best way for a board game to get noticed and accepted is if it's exciting, with lots of moving plastic parts that make noise. Should it be illustrated? Cartoony? What's the theme? Are the rules simple and straightforward? Is there enough going on to satisfy players for 20 minutes to an hour? If you've decided to freelance as a designer, here's how it goes: First, you'll need to make a rough prototype of your game, with some tokens, dice, and cards. You can just borrow parts from another

AT A GLANCE

Salary range
$50,000 to $100,000 and up for a company designer; freelancers typically get a small advance plus royalties, which can be significant if the game is successful.

Education/Experience
Game designers need experience in art and design as well as strong digital-media skills.

Personal Attributes
Skills in design and art, as well as a great deal of originality in ideas and design.

Requirements
None.

Outlook
Fair. Because of the proliferation of electronic games, board game designing jobs are not as plentiful, and competition will continue to tighten.

board game, and use index cards for cards or print your own on business card stock. For the board, you can start with a big sheet of construction paper over an old game board, or go to a copy store for a blowup of your computer graphics. Write down the rules and clarify them as necessary.

If your goal is to sell your invention to a game company, then the prototype needs to clearly communicate fun and innovation. If you want to manufacture the game yourself, you need to figure out the final look of the entire product. Once you've worked out the details of your game, you need to file a patent application for your game to get legal protection for your property. Now you either license the game to a

Jason Schneider, board game designer

Jason Schneider says he was the kid who was always organizing games at his house—and board games were always a very popular choice. Now head of product development and marketing manager at Gamewright of Watertown, Massachusetts (http://www.gamewright.com), Schneider spends every day helping to design or adapt board games for his company. If you've ever played *Slamwich, Scrambled States of America,* or *Rat-a-Tat-Cat,* you've played one of his creations. He's also bringing out a line of fast "12-minute games" that can be played in a short amount of time.

His degree in philosophy from Brandeis gave him a strong analytical background, he says, that helps him now. "Do whatever your heart and conscience tells you to do," he advises kids today. "You'll find the right path. I was fortunate to have supportive parents when I decided to do untraditional things."

Those "untraditional things" started right after graduation, when Schneider went to clown school for the Ringling Bros. Circus. From there, he moved on to a job as child talent coordinator for *Sesame Street,* and then moved to Boston to work for WGBH-TV on the kids' program, *ZOOM!*

Today, he meets with inventors from around the world to track the most interesting and innovative concepts for board games, reviewing and testing games from all different markets for the traditional family game market. "I'm part of the entire process," he says, "from the inception, to the name, even helping with consumer game-play [consumer game testing]."

Schneider's dream is to show children that there's more to life than computers and TV, that playing face to face with each other provides a special interaction missing from electronic games played solo or side by side. "There's such incredible competition from movies, 3-D video, and computer games," he says. "There are so many forms of entertainment out there today. I'm trying to show people there's a whole world out there. Therein lies the challenge."

He spends some time at trade shows, seeing how his games are accepted. "I like seeing my games being enjoyed by people," he says. "Kids will tell you exactly what they think. It's nice to see something you've worked on strike a nerve."

game manufacturer or manufacture it yourself.

If you choose to license the game to a manufacturer, you can either submit it yourself, or use an agent (that's the preferred route). If you want to manufacture the game yourself, you have to choose a distributor—either big chains (such as Toys R Us) or specialty shops. If you pitch to small local stores, and the product sells well, you can eventually buy a booth at a trade show (such as Toy Fair). Trade shows are a good way to meet specialty shop owners; once the game sells well in specialty outlets, the big chains may place orders or ask to license your game.

Most major game manufacturers don't accept unsolicited submissions unless they come through an agent or from an established inventor. For example, Hasbro gets 1,600 submissions a year, and buys no more than 30. Most toy stores have only enough shelf space for established games; bringing in a new game means dropping an old one.

Pitfalls

It's hard to find a job as board game designer in a corporation today; most are freelancers, which means a life of solitary work. If you're a people person, you won't get much interaction with others.

Perks

Working as a board game designer can be a lot of fun. You may get to travel around the world and spend lots of time thinking up creative ways to help others have a good time.

Get a Jump on the Job

Joining gaming groups helps game designers learn which features of games people like and can provide good experience in board game design. Check out the Web site of the Board Game Designers Forum at http://www.bgdf.com or check out the Web site for Board Game Invention at http://spotlightongames.com/list/design .html.

BOOKBINDER

OVERVIEW

If you've ever opened an old, valuable book and been entranced by the marbleized inside covers, you're holding a book hand bound by an artist. Bookbinding is the process of combining printed sheets into finished products, using cutting, folding, gathering, gluing, stapling, stitching, trimming, sewing, wrapping, and other finishing operations.

Job binding workers bind books produced in smaller quantities. In firms specializing in library binding, workers repair books and provide other specialized binding services to libraries. *Blankbook binding* workers bind blank pages to produce notebooks, checkbooks, address books, diaries, calendars, and note pads. Some types of binding and finishing consist of only one step.

Bookbinders assemble books and magazines from large, flat, printed sheets of paper. Skilled workers operate machines that first fold printed sheets into *signatures*, which are groups of pages arranged sequentially. Bookbinders then sew, stitch, or glue the assembled signatures together, shape the book bodies with presses and trimming machines, and reinforce them with glued fabric strips. Covers are created separately, and glued, pasted, or stitched onto the book bodies. The books then undergo a variety of finishing operations, often including wrapping in paper jackets.

A small number of bookbinders work in hand binderies. These highly skilled workers design original or special bindings for limited editions, or restore and rebind rare books. The work requires creativity,

AT A GLANCE

Salary Range

Median hourly earnings of bookbinders range from less than $7.84 to more than $21.90.

Education/Experience

Most bookbinders train on the job. Bindery workers need basic mathematics and language skills, and graphic arts training can be an asset. Vocational-technical institutes offer postsecondary programs in graphic arts, as do some community colleges. Four-year colleges also offer programs, but their emphasis is on preparing people for careers as graphic artists, educators, or managers in the graphic arts field.

Personal Attributes

Bindery work requires careful attention to detail; accuracy, patience, neatness, and good eyesight are also important. Manual dexterity is essential in order to count, insert, paste, and fold. Artistic ability and imagination are necessary.

Requirements

None.

Outlook

Employment for hand bookbinders is expected to decline, reflecting increasingly productive bindery operations, changing business practices, and competition from imports. Opportunities for hand bookbinders are limited because only a small number of establishments do this highly specialized work.

knowledge of binding materials, and a thorough background in the history of binding. Hand bookbinding gives individuals the opportunity to work in the greatest variety of bindery jobs. Bookbinders in small shops may perform many binding tasks, while those in large shops are usually assigned only one or a few operations, such as running complicated manual or

William Streeter, bookbinder

A lifelong interest in Early American industries and town history turned into a career for William Streeter of Northampton, Massachusetts—an accomplished hand bookbinder and coauthor/researcher of three books. During his research for his municipal history books, Streeter discovered many deteriorating church, county, and town records.

Out of desperation, Streeter began meeting with hand bookbinders in Massachusetts, eventually becoming interested in the binding process himself. After apprenticing with binders Lisa Callaway, David Bourbeau, and Daniel Kelm, he opened the Silver Maple Bindery with his wife Elaine in 1982. Soon, he was teaching bookbinding as well, drawing students from all over the country for a full-time three-month course.

Streeter restores many books of sentimental value, such as photo albums, children's books, and family Bibles—so many family Bibles, in fact, that he's often been referred to as "Bible Bill." In addition, his binder can repair torn pages, signatures, and missing pieces, with Japanese tissues of a complementary color and weight to restore integrity and function to the pages. Broken headcaps and corners can be mended with cloth, leather or Japanese tissue. If a book's sewing thread has broken, it can be resewn with linen thread; damaged cords and tapes will be replaced as well, if necessary. If a book's covers and spine have become detached, they can be reattached by placing new cloth, leather, or paper under the original material to form a new spine. Interior hinging will be added or strengthened as part of this process. If a book's binding has deteriorated so much that it is not possible to restore it, it can be re-bound in a period-appropriate cloth, paper, or leather case.

New leather or paper labels can be made to replace torn or missing labels on single or multiple volumes, using genuine gold foil and a variety of typefaces to match original type as closely as possible. The bindery can also produce new covers, monograms, and bookcases.

Streeter loves the camaraderie with his clients, and compares the atmosphere of his bindery to his old general store. After years of working at a variety of jobs, from leatherworker to proprietor of a general store, "Bookbinding is my favorite career of all," says Streeter.

electronic guillotine papercutters or folding machines. Others specialize in adjusting and preparing equipment, and may perform minor repairs as needed.

Most bookbinders learn the craft through on the job training. Inexperienced workers are usually assigned simple tasks such as moving paper from cutting machines to folding machines. They learn basic binding skills, including the characteristics of paper and how to cut large sheets of paper into different sizes with the least amount of waste. As workers gain experience, they advance to more difficult tasks, such as embossing and adding holograms, and learn to operate one or more pieces of equipment. Usually, it takes one to three months to learn to operate the simpler machines but it can take up to one year to become completely familiar with more complex equipment, such as computerized binding machines. Formal apprenticeships are not as common as they used to be, but are still offered by some employers. Apprenticeships provide a more structured program that enables workers to acquire the high levels of specialization and skill needed for some bindery jobs. For example, a four-year apprenticeship is usually necessary to teach workers how to restore rare books and to produce valuable collectors' items.

Computers have caused binding to become increasingly automated. New computer-operated "in-line" equipment performs a number of operations in sequence, beginning with raw stock and ending with a finished product. Technological advances such as automatic tabbers, counters, palletizers, and joggers reduce labor and improve the appearance of the finished product. These improvements are inducing printing companies to acquire in-house binding and finishing equipment that allows printing machine operators to perform bindery work during downtime.

Pitfalls

As self-employed workers, bookbinders must keep up with paperwork, managing their customer base and taxes, in addition to being creative.

Perks

As with most creative jobs, the personal satisfaction of handling old books and creating beautiful bindings for these volumes offsets the difficulties in making a living at this craft.

Get a Jump on the Job

High school students interested in bookbinding careers should take shop courses or attend a vocational-technical high school. Occupational skill centers, usually operated by labor unions, also provide an introduction to a bindery career. To keep pace with changing technology, retraining is increasingly important for bindery workers. Students with computer skills and mechanical aptitude are especially in demand.

BUMPER STICKER WRITER

OVERVIEW

Short-form writing—the fancy term for those pithy sayings emblazoned on everything from bumper stickers to magnets, welcome mats, aprons, key chains, plaques, buttons, and mugs—is a great way to make some extra cash and have a lot of fun all at the same time.

When most folks think of short-form writing, they tend to think of wacky, wild witticisms—and that's the kind of writing companies want for certain products, such as buttons, magnets, and bumper stickers. But other companies who produce plaques and posters may prefer to delve into inspirational, poetic, and dramatic messages. Some are R-rated, some are Christian, some are designed for kids or teens, and some are political. All are tons of fun to create.

So what exactly does a short-form writer do? First, if you decide to specialize in this type of writing, there are some basics. Most companies want to see about 10 slogan ideas typed out on a single page, along with your name and address. You'll need to take a look at a company's Web site or their products in stores to get an idea of the type of humor they use. (It ranges from cutesy, G-rated snippets to raunchy, X-rated phrases.) Some companies have particular topics of interest, such as politics, environmental issues, women-centered humor, parenthood, fishing, golf, and so on. Study what's out there. Go visit gift shops and card shops to see what's selling.

Once you've scoped out the competition, you create a list of about 10 to 20 ideas and send them to the companies, usually by e-mail. These days, few short-form writers bother with the U.S. postal service.

Then, you wait. Sometimes companies respond within a matter of days, and sometimes it takes months. Several companies gather up all their submissions and make decisions only a few times a year for their new catalogs.

Writers who do best in this specialized field are those who are truly original, or who have a unique way of looking at life. Find topics that many people can relate to and then spin them in a short, catchy way. Then ask yourself: *Would I wear a*

Janna Glatzer, short humor writer

Janna Glatzer got started in the bumper sticker biz by entering a contest, on a whim, for greeting card writers—and she won! The prize was an online course with Sandra Miller-Louden, an award-winning greeting card writer and teacher, where Glatzer learned all about the business and craft of writing for the short humor field. Glatzer discovered there was a big market for people who can write catchy short humor for products ranging from bumper stickers, magnets, and doormats to aprons, T-shirts, and keychains.

"I began sending my work out and got a huge kick from seeing it get published!" Glatzer recalls. "There's nothing cooler than having a doormat in front of your house with something you wrote on it!"

Although there are a few companies that come to Glatzer with assignments, she is primarily a freelancer, coming up with lists of ideas and sending them out on speculation.

"The cool thing about short humor is that the ideas pop up everywhere, often from conversations," she says. "If I'm talking to my husband or a friend and either one of us says something funny, that's fodder for my work. I research the companies to see what they're looking for, and I purposely keep my brain attuned to humor in those categories."

For example, she explains, High Cotton (a gift manufacturer) uses fishing-related humor. Both Glatzer's husband and father are fishermen, so she pays attention to their expeditions and mines their experiences for humorous ideas. She brainstorms on the topic to find related words. If she's brainstorming about fishing, she might make up a list that looks like this:

Worms … Smelly … Hook … Sinker … Catching … Boat … Bait … Pole

When she has five free minutes, she sits with that list and sees if anything inspires her to create. Here are some samples of Glatzer's short humor that she has sold to a variety of companies: "I cook, therefore you clean" (for an apron); "We love our vacuum, we've found God, and we gave at the office. Thank you." (doormat); "Set the table quietly and no one will get hurt" (apron).

"It's a total trip to have my humor appear on products people wear and use," Glatzer says. "It's also the kind of work you can do in your spare time. You don't need to have hours free to sit down and work on this; it's great for people with short attention spans."

Short humor isn't always a lot of laughs, Glatzer notes. It can be frustrating for her to come up with the funniest idea ever, and then not be able to find anyone to buy it—yet companies line up to purchase some of her less-favorite ideas. "Sometimes I'll send out a list of 20 ideas to a company and sell three of them for $150 apiece," she says. "Sometimes I'll completely bomb and sell nothing in a batch."

In addition to her short-form writing, Jenna Glatzer is editor-in-chief of AbsoluteWrite.com, a popular online magazine for writers. She's also the author of *Make a Real Living as a Freelance Writer* and *Outwitting Writer's Block and Other Problems of the Pen,* among other books. Visit her Web site at http://www.jennaglatzer.com for more info and to find some free goodies!

button that says what I'm proposing? Would I put this bumper sticker on my car or plop that doormat on my front porch?

Funny isn't enough, all on its own. There has to be something about it that will make people want to plunk down their hard-earned cash on it, and use it, wear it, or give it as a gift. People rarely buy jokes just for the sake of jokes; they buy funny stuff that speaks to them on some level, or that defines their identity—as a mom, a Democrat, a punk, a feminist, an anarchist, a bride-to-be... whatever.

Pitfalls

Most slogan writers freelance, so if you want to write bumper stickers or magnet slogans you'll probably be self-employed. This can mean uneven income, no benefits, and no paid vacations.

Perks

Getting to sit around all day thinking up wacky slogans—and getting paid for it—can be an enormously fun, rewarding way to make a living. Truly gifted bumper sticker writers can make quite a bit of money if they can manage to sell on a continuing basis.

Get a Jump on the Job

You don't need a college degree for this, so if you think you'd like to try your hand at short-form writing, just start brainstorming and submit your work. *Writer's Market* (an annual guide by Writer's Digest Books) also lists many markets for this kind of work. Consider taking a short-form humor-writing course with Sandra Miller-Louden, an award-winning greeting card writer and teacher, at http://www.absolutewrite.com/classes/Louden/greetingcards.htm. There's also a message board there for people who write greeting cards and product slogans, at http://absolutewrite.com/forums.

CALLIGRAPHER

OVERVIEW

The word *calligraphy* comes from the Greek words, *kalli*, meaning beautiful, and *graphia*, meaning writing. Therefore, a calligrapher is an artist who specializes in beautiful writing. Basically, you get the effect of calligraphy, or decorative writing, by using pens with different tips that make wide vertical strokes and narrow horizontal strokes. Calligraphy was a popular pastime as far back as prehistoric cavedwellers—and it's been around ever since, despite threats to its existence from the printing press in the 15th century. Today, calligraphy has evolved into a respected visual art form, and calligraphers have formed guilds and societies to celebrate their work.

If you choose calligraphy as a profession, you will probably be working special occasions and events, such as invitations to weddings and special parties, menus from fancy restaurants, and birth announcements, along with certificates, place mats and personalized greeting cards. You might find yourself working directly with clients or developing relationships with stationary stores, wedding planners, printers, or design agencies. The advantage of having a relationship with a store or agency is that you're likely to get a steady stream of jobs. The downside is that you may not be able to pick and choose your jobs as you could if you were on your own.

To get started as a calligrapher, you've got to have samples of your work to show prospective clients. Make your own business card, being sure the design

reflects your talent. If you're going to go after clients directly, you'll have to come up with a business plan that includes how you're going to market yourself and your work.

Because networking is important in a business such as calligraphy, you can join an artist's guild in your area or try to find out if there are any groups or societies of calligraphers. And remember that clients who pay for calligraphy services expect the work to be done as specified and completed on time. It would be disastrous to your business to have to tell a client that her wedding invitations can't be mailed out on time because you didn't finish your work as scheduled.

Nan DeLuca, calligrapher

Nan DeLuca, owner of Calligraphy by Nan DeLuca in New York City, has been a full-time calligrapher for 10 years, and she's well known for her work. Her wedding invitations have been featured in publications such as *Martha Stewart Weddings* and *InStyle Weddings* and on the TV show *Entertainment Weekly*. While she enjoys her work and the acclaim that comes with it, she never stops learning and working to improve her skills.

"I still take classes," she says. "There are always others more skilled than I to learn from, different styles to learn, and more tricks to acquire."

DeLuca has an art background, but she wasn't working in the field during the years she was raising her children. As they got older, she started looking for a creative outlet and discovered calligraphy. She took evening and weekend classes and did calligraphy for her children's friends and schools. When someone asked her to address wedding invitations in calligraphy, she hesitated, but ultimately agreed, kicking off a career that has flourished ever since.

While most of DeLuca's clients are referrals from satisfied customers, she also markets herself on her Web site and provides free work for photo shoots and printers, which allows others to see her calligraphy. She's also very active in the New York City–based Society of Scribes, an association of calligraphers. DeLuca strongly advises anyone looking to be a calligrapher to find a good teacher.

"Books are nice, but there is no substitute for someone teaching you to hold the pen right, how to make the letterforms correctly, and how to 'see' the letters form on the page," she said. "Otherwise, you can practice for hours and hours and never know if you are just ingraining mistakes rather than improving. It is not just the hand that needs training, it's the eye."

She also recommends using the Internet to find calligraphy groups and organizations (see Appendix A) and studying calligraphy books to get a better idea of different forms of the art. Above all: Be patient! "Calligraphy is not an instantly learned art," she explains. "Many—if not all of us— study for years and keep on taking more classes just to improve."

Pitfalls

While there are jobs and opportunities for calligraphers, many people are now designing their own invitations and cards on their home computers. As a result, competition for calligraphy jobs is apt to be keen. There's also a fair amount of stress on this job, since one misspelled name or misplaced number could ruin an entire job.

Perks

If you love the art of calligraphy, what could be better than earning money as a calligrapher? Many calligraphers rejoice in their art and get great satisfaction from it. Chances are good that you can set your own work hours and, as your business grows, pick and choose the jobs that you want to do.

Get a Jump on the Job

There are many teach-yourself calligraphy kits available and courses at local art schools, technical centers, and community colleges. Join an artist's guild or calligrapher society and ask for advice from other members.

CARICATURIST

OVERVIEW

Have you ever been to a theme park and watched a caricaturist create an amazing likeness with a few quick strokes from his pencil? Caricaturists are a lot like cartoonists, but with a special knack for emphasizing facial and body features in order to create a comic but completely recognizable drawing. Being able to draw portraits of people and knowing and understanding the human face is central to being able to draw a caricature.

The successful caricaturist tries to distort a person's looks without getting too far away from what the person sees in him- or herself. The drawing should be an exaggeration and perhaps a little bit insulting, but never downright cruel. Getting this exaggeration just right can be challenging, however, because a person's features are what makes him recognizable. When you start changing these features, you run the risk of losing the likeness. The trick is to play down a person's minor features and emphasize prominent ones.

To start doing caricature, you'll need to get a hard surface on which to draw, some typing paper (at least 8.5 x 11 inches), a pink school eraser, and a couple of 5B or 4B pencils. (The lead in number 2 pencils is too hard to make a good drawing.) You may also want to get a blending tool to help create shadows quickly.

Unlike portraiture, caricaturing should have an element of cartooning to it, with simple, bold lines. The lines you draw should really separate one element from another and be dark and confident. Be confident in your lines and don't timidly sketch them. Be bold!

AT A GLANCE

Salary Range
Varies considerably depending on area and type; retail income is about $20 per drawing; an event runs between $50 to $150 an hour.

Education/Experience
A degree in art is helpful, although most art schools don't have a major in caricature.

Personal Attributes
Excellent people and entertainment skills, ability to draw well and quickly and to work hard.

Requirements
Artistic ability, outgoing personality.

Outlook
Excellent. There are many opportunities for caricaturists, both in retail (such as theme parks and outdoor fairs) and in entertainment (such as trade shows and parties).

Caricaturists work as freelancers, or for concessionaires at theme parks and outdoor events. To succeed in this business, you've got to be good at quickly capturing someone's likeness and exaggerating some aspect of their appearance—but not highlighting someone's bad points so well that the experience becomes insulting. Ultimately, the customer chooses whether or not to pay for the caricature, and if you've made the drawing so unappealing or unattractive that it's upsetting, you'll lose the sale.

In addition to working at concession stands at theme parks (or *retail*, as it's called), more and more caricaturists are finding work as entertainers at parties and corporate conventions and trade shows. Those who work as a caricaturist entertainer at parties or conventions need to be not just good artists, but also

Keelan Parham, caricaturist

Keelan Parham always thought he'd be a world-famous comic book artist. But art schools at the time never taught even one class in caricature; at the Savannah College of Art and Design, professors tried to pigeonhole Parham as either a graphics or fine arts major.

He was neither.

After graduation, he worked as a model and actor until a fateful visit to Orlando, where he answered an ad for a caricaturist at Walt Disney World. Caricature concessions aren't run by Disney, but by independent business owners who contract with the theme park to provide caricaturists. Parham's new boss started him off without any training at all, and it was a rude awakening for the young artist. "I was literally thrown to the sharks," he recalls. "I was so terrified." For the entire first week, he spent the time watching others and didn't draw one caricature. Eventually, of course, he picked up a pencil and began, and once he started, he was hooked.

Today, he owns the primary caricature concession at Walt Disney World, employing 30 artists, and also owns a caricature business (Caricature Connection at http://www.caricatureconnection.com) that handles retail and entertainment caricature bookings all over the country, as well as mail orders. For himself, he draws mostly at entertainment bookings—parties, conventions, trade shows, banquets, company parties, picnics, grand openings, tournaments, parties, and lots and lots of weddings at Walt Disney World. His corporate clients include everyone from Aetna to Xerox, and just about every major company in between, including Bayer, Coke, Exxon, McDonald's, and NBC. He has also written a how-to for prospective caricature artists: *Let's Toon Caricatures.*

With all those hours spent caricaturing others, is he ever tempted to draw himself? "People always ask me that," he laughs. "But I always want to draw myself better looking than I really am."

As much as people don't like the way they look, they love to have their picture drawn, he's discovered. "It's interesting to me, how much people love caricatures. I could relocate to Iowa and make a good living on the street corner, drawing caricatures.

"People rarely realize what they look like. In fact, my most successful caricature is the one that the person doesn't like. I wish I had known about caricatures long ago," he says. "I love my work. As long as people are laughing, I've done my job."

outgoing individuals able to entertain a crowd with some fancy pencilwork. At these events, the caricaturist is really trying to please an audience, rather than worrying about whether the person who is being drawn likes the final product. Because it's the folks watching over the caricaturist's shoulder who really count in this setting, the caricature can be more exaggerated and emphasize a person's features. It's still a good idea to stop short of being completely insulting. In this case, making sure the crowd is laughing and enjoying themselves is the key.

Although there are plenty of caricaturists at work around the country, you won't find an art school anywhere that offers a major in this art form. However, more and more schools are beginning to offer caricature courses and workshops.

Pitfalls

Dealing with people can be stressful, especially because most people don't really know what they look like, and therefore tend not to recognize themselves in the drawing. Artists who aren't comfortable with people looking over their shoulder while they work will have trouble working as a caricaturist.

Perks

An artist can make a very good living while maintaining independence. The job is always different and always changing. More outgoing artists who genuinely enjoy interacting with people will thrive in this career.

Get a Jump on the Job

The best way to prepare for a job as a caricature is to draw every day. Practice drawing shapes, and look for shapes in everything around you. Get a good book about caricature to look for tips on how to create this special type of art (see Read More About It at the end of this book for some good books). And practice, practice, practice!

CATALOG COPYWRITER

OVERVIEW

If you can turn a description of a simple piece of luggage into a paean to international travel, you might have the makings of a top-notch catalog copywriter. These writing experts are adept at churning out snappy prose and witty descriptions at a rapid pace, making a company's products irresistible to its potential customers.

When new products are introduced that need to be added to the catalog, it's the catalog copywriter who's called in to convince the customer that the item is a must-have. Exactly how the writer chooses to do this depends in large part on the company's attitude and reputation—how it sees itself and its customers. The advertising patter for a writer at Victoria's Secret would be quite different from the copy produced for Land's End, for example.

First, the copywriter starts with a headline carefully crafted to catch the reader's attention. For example, a recent Orvis catalog snags readers' interest with this headline: "Organization for every room." Under that encouraging headline is a blurb for a bill-payer's desk: "Why not make the unpleasant task of paying bills more organized?" the catalog invites, going on to extol the benefits of this new piece of furniture.

Each headline is matched to the type of sell the catalog is aiming for. Next, the copywriter tries to use phrases that stimulate the senses and pack a lot

AT A GLANCE

Salary Range
$24,000 to $90,000+

Education/Experience
College degree required (journalism, writing, or advertising major helpful).

Personal Attributes
Good writing skills, creativity, persuasiveness.

Requirements
None.

Outlook
While this field is competitive, there are many job opportunities in a variety of settings, both corporate and freelance. Most chances of employment can be found in larger cities, such as New York, Boston, Los Angeles, and Chicago.

of punch with an economy of words. Although it's much easier to write long than to write short and tight, the job of a good catalog copywriter is to condense a world of meaning into a few short phrases.

A degree in advertising, public relations, marketing, or journalism can provide you with the basics, but what's most important is writing experience, and plenty of experience reading catalogs. You can read all the "how to be a great copywriter" books there are, but the best way to improve copywriting skills is to read specialty catalogs that offer current examples of the best (and worst) in copywriting. You'll get more from a 30-minute study of an Orvis or L.L. Bean catalog than from any copywriting textbook ever written. (Not to mention the fact that catalogs are free!)

Veronique McAree, catalog copywriter

If you've ever spent time perusing the beautifully photographed catalogs of L.L. Bean, filled with pictures of people wearing handsome, sporty clothes and playing with adorable golden retrievers, you may very well have come across the work of Veronique McAree.

McAree, an editorial manager at L.L. Bean, is responsible for coming up with the many of the descriptions of items the Maine company offers for sale.

"We're trying to give the customer a reason to buy," McAree explains. "We try to explain how the product can have impact in practical ways, and how it can add relevance to their lives."

McAree started out her writing career armed with a journalism degree and experience in the New York City women's magazine publishing world. But a writing degree isn't a requirement at L.L. Bean; many other catalog copywriters have come from a variety of related backgrounds, such as public relations, advertising, and marketing.

A typical day might begin at a product turnover meeting, where copywriters get to see and touch the new products and read the specific information on each item. How many words a copywriter has to come up with for each product depends on what it is: A simple sweater might not require nearly as much space as a "hero product" would—one the company is forecasting as a potential big seller.

To enliven their catalogs, copywriters may be called on to create 500-word articles to go along with certain products, McAree explains. She specializes in outdoor and travel items.

Writers who might be stumped at how to handle a certain product can go back to the company archives—all the way back to 1912—and see how former colleagues might have handled the writing. "There's a true heritage here," McAree explains, "and a practical approach to writing."

For young writers, catalog copywriting can be a nice stepping-stone to other things, providing training in tracking down details and learning how to tell a story, as well as learning about the business world.

"I would say it can never hurt to have a strong writing background," McAree advises. "In college, learn about marketing, business, and how to tell a story about a product."

Pitfalls

Constant deadlines can be a major headache in larger firms that bring out many catalogs a year, and the constant pressure to come up with catchy phrases can be stressful.

Perks

If you enjoy writing and you've got a knack for great descriptions, this sort of job can be enormously interesting, always different, and lucrative. It takes a unique skill to be able to describe something in just a few hundred words, and to make it so compelling that customers will want to buy that product.

Get a Jump on the Job

Write every day. Practice trying to condense your writing and hone your skills at being descriptive yet succinct. Look around your room and start writing pretend ads for your favorite brand of jeans or a great CD. Read lots of catalogs and books on the advertising industry.

CLOTHING PATTERNMAKER

OVERVIEW

If you love fashion, being a patternmaker gives you a front row seat to the latest designs and styles. Clothing patternmakers are an important part of the apparel industry. Without patternmakers, new styles of clothing couldn't be manufactured. Taking the ideas of a fashion designer, a patternmaker draws outlines of clothing and then cuts full-size patterns from paper, fiberboard, or fabric. Patterns often are made in sections, called *blocks*. Patternmakers are required to mark their work with sewing instructions and codes, and to work with a team of people to produce a sample garment. It's then the job of the patternmaker to correct any errors in the garment, and to make adjustments if the pattern doesn't comply with the clothing design.

As a patternmaker, you're among the first to see clothing designs, and once you're established it's likely that your opinions about design changes and alterations will be welcomed. Because patternmakers understand the technical aspect of a design, they are often called on to act as liaisons between clothing designers and clothing manufacturers.

Organizational skills are important for a patternmaker, who often faces tight deadlines and must coordinate working with different teams of people. Being able to communicate effectively with designers and clothing manufacturers also is vital to your success. If you've always hated math, you might want to reconsider a career in patternmaking, as it involves math formulas and equations. Computers are increasingly

AT A GLANCE

Salary Range

$25,000 to $150,000 a year, depending on experience and area of employment. Average salary about $75,000.

Education/Experience

Associate of arts degree in fashion design and patternmaking from a vocational school or school specializing in fashion and design. An apprenticeship with an experienced patternmaker is extremely useful; experience in design or retail work is also beneficial. Sewing machine skills are crucial.

Personal Attributes

Accurate and neat, with good hand-eye coordination, a good sense of body proportions, and the ability to use drafting tools and computer-aided design (CAD) equipment. It's important to be able to visualize what a garment is to look like, and to communicate ideas effectively with a designer.

Requirements

Some employers will train you, but others—particularly larger companies—require a one- or two-year certificate or a degree from a technical training or vocational school. CAD equipment is being used more and more in patternmaking.

Outlook

Although there is not much anticipated job growth, freelance work may be available by working directly with designers. This could create additional opportunities for patternmakers, and begin a career path toward clothing design.

being used to create patterns, so you should be aware of available CAD programs and know how to use them.

Because the fashion industry is pressured to keep coming out with new products, there is a certain amount of stress for those who work in it—including patternmakers. You'll

Cherie Bixler, clothing patternmaker

Fashion designing lured Cherie Bixler into the fashion business about 23 years ago, but she quickly moved into patternmaking when she realized how competitive the designer market was. After living in New York City for 20 years, she moved back home to Arkansas City, Arkansas, where she now operates a Web-based patternmaking business called Cherie Bixler Pattern Service & Consultants. Bixler has worked for department stores, apparel companies, and mail order catalog companies, as well as individuals who hire her to make patterns for the perfect outfit.

"I love what I do," Bixler said. "It's a great career for someone who doesn't want something that's monotonous, because every pattern I make is different. And it's challenging, so I never get tired of it."

One of the most important qualifications in being a good patternmaker is to know how to sew on a sewing machine, Bixler said. As improbable as it might seem, many people with no sewing experience attempt to enter the industry.

Although most fashion designers and patternmakers are based in cities with a significant fashion industry, Bixler said it's possible to go out on your own, once you've established yourself in the industry. Then you can operate your business from wherever you want or consider a Web-based business, as she has.

probably face some tight deadlines, and may be required to work overtime during peak periods. Also, as in many industries, there is a certain hierarchy in the fashion world. As a patternmaker, you may need to establish yourself in order to gain credibility with those who hold different jobs within the industry.

Pitfalls

You may have to work long hours during busy seasons, and you may have to learn to be adaptable about your working location and conditions. Patternmakers often spend hours at a time working on computers or standing over a table containing pattern pieces. And because you'll work with designers and clothing makers, you'll need to move around to accommodate them. You may have to work extra hours on your own to keep up with changing computer programs.

Perks

Clothing companies realize the importance of patternmakers, and most large companies are willing to pay them well; their work is recognized and valued. If you land a job with a major apparel firm, you'll have opportunity for advancement and could earn a fairly high salary. And once you're established as a patternmaker and have some experience, it's likely that you'll be able to find freelance work if you want to. Eventually, you could end up picking and choosing jobs and perhaps even starting your own business.

Get a Jump On the Job

If you're enrolled in a fashion, technical, or vocational school, ask your career counselor if there are any internships available. If you don't have any fashion-related experience, look for a job that will expose you to some aspect of the fashion industry—even if it's working in a clothing store or clothing department of a department store.

COSTUME DESIGNER

OVERVIEW

Whether it's the feline perfection of the actors in *CATS*, the leonine grace of the *Lion King* puppets, or the period authenticity of the *Titanic* evening wear, the costume designer is an artist who brings the music, dance, or script to life. It's a profoundly creative career steeped in exhaustive research and extensive knowledge of color, fabric, and style.

Every garment worn in a theatrical or musical production is a costume. Before an actor opens his mouth, his clothing has already spoken for him. From the most obvious and flamboyant outfits, to contemporary clothing using subtle design language, costume design plays an integral part in every ballet, every musical, and every TV and film production. It is an ancient theatrical craft and a vital tool for storytelling.

Much of the costume designer's art the public never sees. For example, in director M. Night Shyamalan's *The Village*, it's not just the color of the costumes or the style that's important—the costume designer had to decide whether early Pennsylvania settlers would use bone, shell, or wooden buttons, zippers or clasps, linen or cotton. If linen, settlers must be shown to grow flax; if wool, they must have sheep to shear. Would viewers notice—or care—that the actors were wearing metal instead of wooden buttons? No. But the costume designer does care, because such attention to detail lends authenticity to the production.

To this end, costume designers (and their assistants and associates) endlessly research and design authentic costumes true to period, country, and social class. They can be found working for films, TV, opera, ballet, concerts, and stage companies. Costume designers are passionate storytellers, historians, social commentators, trendsetters, magicians, and project managers, who must juggle shrinking wardrobe budgets and tight-fisted producers.

If you were a costume designer just hired to work on a movie, you'd be given a script to read over to absorb the mood, time period, and setting in which the action occurs. Then comes the research, sketches of costumes, and development of costume budgets for the entire production. How many costume changes are required for each of the actors? How many boots, hats, and gloves? A good costume designer plays a big part in bringing characters or time periods to vivid life on stage or screen.

As a costume designer, you would work closely with the production designer and director to establish the visual requirements of the script in pre-production, making sure the colors and imagery blend. If it's a period production, you'll need to ensure that costumes are historically accurate, and you'll have to break down the script to establish the number of costumes and changes of costume that each actor will require.

Then, you help plan, design, and supervise the purchase, hiring, or creation of all costumes for the production—from shoes to hats, including gloves, dresses, cloaks, and even undergarments. Next, you'll work with the heads of department of wardrobe, hair, and makeup and supervise costume fittings at rehearsals with the director to ensure the overall look will be right.

If you're working on a film, you're required to be on set as each new scene is begun. If you've done your homework, the costumes are accepted by the director, but if anything in the scene changes, the costumes also may need to be altered. The costume designer works ahead, fitting and preparing costumes and ensuring everything required is available when scheduled for filming.

Costume designers are also responsible for lots of paperwork related to the costume department, and they need to keep track of the condition of what's available, and then select, procure, fit, alter, and clean costumes for cast members.

Designers also review scripts and study books, pictures, and examples of costumes as well as determine how many costumes are needed for each character. Tracking inventory is also very important for this occupation. Costume designers deal with hundreds of costumes for some productions, so keeping track of all the outfits is no small chore.

When a costume designer receives a script, the process of developing the visual shorthand for each character begins. Costume sketches, fashion research, and actual garments are used to help costume designers, directors, and actors develop a common language for the development of each character. Sometimes a glamorous entrance may be inappropriate and destructive to a scene. The costume designer must first serve the story and the director.

The more specific and articulate a costume is, the more effective it will be with an audience. Minute details loved by actors often enhance their performances in imperceptible ways. In fact, many actors say their costume helped them discover their characters.

Costumes have always had enormous influence on the world of fashion. A style cycle begins as a famous actor's role is recreated in retail fashion; the exposure this celebrity brings to a costume can generate millions of dollars for the fashion business. Costume designers receive

Mitchell Bloom, associate costume designer

He's worked in just about every entertainment venue there is—ballet, opera, Broadway, movies, TV—designing costumes for everyone from Woody Allen to Bernadette Peters.

But what he likes best about costume design is the research: What were real people wearing during that time period? How did they look? And will that look translate well onto 21st-century actors onstage?

For Mitchell Bloom, freelance associate costume designer in New York City, it's all in a day's work. "Every job lends itself to different things. Is it a period piece? An adaptation from a novel? A transfer from London? I like that it's a collaboration, and it's always different." Each job also usually has its own set of problems.

"[The film] *The Village* had its own set of problems," he notes. "There was 'good color' and 'bad color' [for good and bad characters]—there were only two colors and they had to be used in a special way."

Bloom advises prospective costume designers to attend a good liberal arts school for a broad education. A Brandeis graduate, Bloom says he had to take math, science, and history in college, and he was all the better for it. "College is not necessarily a trade school," he says. "What I do doesn't really exist as a major in college."

As a boy, Bloom had no interest in theater—he was a Boy Scout, learned woodcarving, made his own moccasins from a kit. "I did every kind of hobby kit craft," he remembers, "along with some art and photography."

Although his mother sewed, he didn't really do any sewing or design until college. "I got my prerequisites out of the way first," he said, "and then I took introduction to physical production, costumes, scenic lighting. I was a stage manager, and I was good at it. People were always asking me to help them with their homework."

His first job after school was as a scene painter. "But having your hand in a bucket of paint is not the healthiest way to live," he notes, and so he moved on to begin working in costumes. For him, it was a natural fit. "The history part I always liked. You get the gig, you read the script, and start doing the research. I have lots of Sears books, gloves, hats, shoes. In high school I bought a box of strange men's linen collars. If you hold onto it long enough, you'll find a use for it."

"I find often that pictures of people in real settings are better than catalogs," he notes.

tremendous pride from seeing their efforts reproduced on a huge scale, but typically get little recognition and no renumeration for setting worldwide trends.

So how do you get started? There are various routes into the profession—some people get experience as design assistants in the wardrobe departments of theaters, or work in the fashion industry, or attend art school. Opportunities exist in most theaters that present their own productions, along with an increasing number of independent film and TV production companies and production companies making ads and videos.

Many successful costume designers are self-employed, working on a freelance basis or as a consultant.

Pitfalls

The work of a costume designer can be enormously stressful and very, very hard, with extremely long hours.

Pay in the beginning isn't good, he notes. In the 1980s, Bloom was making about $185 a week. "You work long hours, and if you're lucky you get one day off a week. People in this business don't seem to retire. They just work and work and work, until they drop dead."

"Last year [2004] was my best year. This year [2005] is my worst in several years; I didn't have full-time work at all in the summer."

If you want to be a costume designer, Bloom suggests that it might be better to take an off-off-off Broadway show, because the producer might be a success, and take you along. If you work for a high-profile show as a costume assistant, they may only think of you as an assistant. Experience, he believes, is better than a master's degree.

"I probably work the longest hours of anyone in a show," Bloom says. " I get up at 6 a.m. to be at a fabric store at 8 a.m. And I work all day. Then the theater opens at 6:30 p.m. and the curtain goes up at 8 p.m. I'm in the audience night after night, the curtain comes down at 11 p.m., but then you have to wait for the director to have a meeting, and there are meetings with wardrobe supervisors until midnight."

The ability to work as part of a team is also important. Although you have to take pride in your work, working as a costume designer is a collaborative effort among the director, designer, and producers. "You can't alienate people above or beneath you," Bloom says. "You have to know when to pick your fights."

And everyone has their likes and dislikes. For example, Bloom doesn't like working on modern dress, because everybody has an opinion on what the clothing should look like. "In the *Goodbye Girl* musical, it was a free-for-all," he observes. "The farther away you go from present day, the more people will trust the costume designer. As much as I love research, some things you have to fudge. A real 1920s suit wouldn't fit a modern body. Actors need a certain level of mobility, and an ill-fitting 1920s suit wouldn't look nice to the modern eye."

As creative as this job seems to be, however, Bloom notes that there's also a certain amount of boring paperwork involved: Who's in what scene? How many times do they change clothes? What time of day is it? What year, what location? "You have to time everything with a stopwatch," he says. "Okay, it's six lines of dialogue, how long does that take? You have to chart who's in what scene. It's crazy, but it's also really a lot of fun."

Perks

For those who love art, fabric, research, and clothing design—not to mention the incredible atmosphere of the theater and entertainment world—there can be no more exciting place to be. The job is full of challenges, but every day is different and there's always something new to learn. As you become more successful, you'll also have the chance to work with celebrities, well-known artists, producers, and directors.

Get a Jump on the Job

Get involved in every type of theatrical or musical production you can, working backstage on costumes. Learn to sew and study books on historical costumes and costume design. See if you can work with a costume designer at your local community theater. The more experience you can get, the better!

FINE ARTIST

OVERVIEW

Fine artists might be painters or illustrators who create in order to communicate a feeling, mood, or idea. Their work is found in galleries, museums, homes, and offices. Other fine artists might work as art critics, evaluating art or serving as consultants to foundations that invest in art.

The works of fine artists are as varied as the artists themselves, and include stone carvings, oil paintings, watercolors, etchings in wood or metal, and illustrations for books or magazines. The work of every artist is different, and the value of it subjective. This can make it difficult for the artist to establish a price for a work.

Some artists work on commission—that is, creating works as requested by a client. Others produce works for exhibition and eventual sale. Some artists display work in their studios, while others have other outlets for their work, such as an art shop, restaurant, gallery, or art show.

Most fine artists have formal training, although there are no established requirements for being a fine artist. Many have fine arts degrees from recognized art schools. In addition to art education, however, artists are being increasingly forced to pay attention to the business end of their profession, and many are learning early on that it's not enough to be able to create beautiful works if you want to make a living from your work. You must be able to attract customers, keep track of orders, arrange for your work to be shown, work with gallery owners, shopkeepers, and others, and keep track of other business dealings. Many beginning artists, and those

AT A GLANCE

Salary Range

Wages for a salaried fine artist (that is, someone hired by a company to create artwork) range from less than $16,900 to more than $73,560, with an average of $35,260. The earnings of freelance artists vary tremendously, depending on experience, location, and demand for the work. More than half of all artists work on a freelance basis.

Experience/Education

Most professional artists hold a degree in fine arts or a related area. Studio experience is also necessary.

Personal Attributes

Must be creative, with a sense for color and form. Must be willing to work hard at developing your talent, and must be able to market yourself and your work.

Requirements

A portfolio is necessary, as is training. Knowledge of art history is useful.

Outlook

Employment for fine artists is expected to grow about as fast as the average, between 10 and 20 percent through 2012.

who don't learn to market themselves, are forced to have a second job in order to earn enough money to live on.

Art entails challenges and problems, which artists must be able to creatively address and solve. Patience is a virtue, since you'll often have to analyze various options for problem solving and perhaps try different approaches before you're successful.

Pitfalls

Making fine art requires hard work and concentration, and can be a solitary endeavor. If you don't like working by yourself, you might want to consider an area of art in which there is more opportunity for social interaction, such

Jennifer Takahashi, fine artist

Jennifer Takahashi's interest in art began at an early age, eventually leading her to become a painter—a fine artist who works primarily with watercolors and oils. Takahashi has become recognized for her distinctive style of painting, which is extremely detailed and complex. Her paintings have been exhibited in numerous locations, including New York City art galleries, the lobbies of huge corporate headquarters, libraries, city restaurants, university galleries, and other types of shows and exhibits.

Takahashi's training, education, and hard work, however, began many years before her paintings began appearing in shows and galleries. She took art lessons as a youth and teenager and earned an art degree in college. After graduating, she moved to San Francisco, where she worked as both an animation artist and a fabric designer. The hours were long and the pay minimal, but she was determined to get as much experience as possible.

She and her husband eventually moved back to South Orange, New Jersey, and Takahashi began working with watercolors. At first, her work appeared only at local shows. As her painting style developed and became recognized, however, she found more and more opportunities to display and sell her work. In the 13 years that Takahashi has been working as a fine artist, she has completed 80 paintings, 60 of which she has sold.

"I feel very lucky to be able to do what I do," she says. "There are days that I feel better about my work than others, but I always know that I'm doing something that I love, and being paid to do it."

Getting your work exhibited when you're first starting out can be challenging, Takahashi says, but there are ways to make it happen. She advises looking for juried shows, which are shows that include only the work of artists who make it through a screening process. These shows are advertised in magazines and other publications geared toward artists, she said, and are often held at universities or community centers.

Takahashi also advises would-be artists to seek out and join local and state arts councils, many of which hold shows and provide other benefits for artists. "These groups can provide you with information about events in your area," she says. "And they're valuable networking tools for artists."

Takahashi encourages young artists to be creative, and not be afraid to approach other artists. She belongs to a group of about 35 artists in her area who have formed an artists' cooperative called The Exhibitors Co-op. Strength is in numbers, Takahashi says, and the co-op is able to find space for exhibits where one or two artists never could. For example, it takes a lot of artwork to fill the lobby of a huge pharmaceutical company, but if each member of the co-op contributes three pieces, there's plenty, and the company is much more likely to take an interest. "

It widens your opportunities," Takahashi explains. "Even if you have a co-op of just five or six artists, you have more influence than a single artist."

Once you have a collection of paintings that have been exhibited, you can approach gallery owners with slides of your work and ask if they'd be interested in displaying your work. The advantage to this, Takahashi says, is that many people see your paintings, increasing the chances that someone will buy one. The disadvantage, however, is that you have to share the proceeds of the sale—sometimes as much as 50 percent—with the owner of the gallery.

(continues)

(continued)

"That's really difficult," she says. "You have to know your market. You have to know what the people around you are going to be willing to spend on a painting. When my work was exhibited in New York [City], the gallery owner charged a lot more than I'm comfortable charging in my area. I don't know many people who are willing to pay $12,000 or $15,000 or $20,000 for a painting."

On the other hand, she says, because her paintings are very detailed it can take several months for her to complete one. That means she must be mindful of the time and effort she's spent on a painting when pricing it.

"You know, I can't take my paintings to a street fair, because nobody there would be able to pay me what I need to ask for them," Takahashi says. "On the other hand, I did a whole series of small drawings that I could do quickly, and I did sell them at street fairs. People really liked them, and I sold a lot of them, so that was good too."

Takahashi advises anyone considering a career as a fine artist to get as much training and education as possible, and to experience different types of art by working in different kinds of jobs. Above all, she said, you must be willing to practice and work, and then practice and work some more.

"It's not an easy profession, by any means," she says. "And yet, I feel blessed every day. While it's important to work hard, it's also important to give yourself some breaks. Stretch yourself with some technical and time challenges, and then relax a little and do something that comes a little easier to you. And stay focused."

as teaching or commercial art. You also need to be disciplined to work without supervision.

Perks

If you enjoy working alone and don't have trouble keeping yourself disciplined to work, fine art may be the best thing for you to do. Artists generally find much satisfaction in creating art, and sales of your work can be lucrative once you're established and have built a following.

Get a Jump on the Job

Take art lessons if possible, even if it's at school. If you're really interested in art, chances are that an art teacher in your school will be willing to give you extra help and instruction. Or, there are private art classes available in most communities. Don't be afraid to volunteer to have your work included in school or local exhibits. You might also volunteer to work at art shows within your community, which will give you a chance to meet artists and observe their work. Art shows are usually advertised in local newspapers.

FORENSIC ARTIST

OVERVIEW

You've probably seen their handiwork in a local newspaper in the wake of a crime—a black-and-white drawing of a steely-eyed criminal peering out from the pages of the daily paper.

Forensic drawings like this are typically used not to catch a criminal, but to rule out others who don't look anything like the crook. But very often, when the felon is later apprehended, the photo of the crook and the forensic drawing do appear eerily alike.

Forensic artists provide numerous functions for an agency, including composite drawings of criminals, age progression drawings of missing persons or fleeing felons, and skull reconstructions of unknown murder victims. Most of their work, however, is drawing crooks by plumbing the memories of witnesses.

How can an artist draw a picture of a criminal simply from the description of a witness and have it come out anywhere near a likeness? Years of training, good witness interviewing skills, and artistic talent all help.

A forensic artist is a composite artist. When a crime occurs and there isn't any evidence—but there is a witness—a forensic artist can use his or her drawing skills to create a likeness of the suspect. Although computerized Identikits exist—in which an overlay is built up using standardized facial features—the computer can only use whatever features are in its database.

A forensic artist is limited only by talent and the information he or she can

AT A GLANCE

Salary Range

$19,000 to $42,000+ annually; $200 to $1,000 per portrait, freelance.

Education/Experience

Art degree helpful but not required; courses in composite art or forensic art vital; apprenticeship helpful.

Personal Attributes

Artistic talent, good communication and interview skills.

Requirements

None.

Outlook

Fairly difficult to find full-time forensic artist work (except in very large city police departments); perseverance can pay off.

extract from a witness. In fact, a talented forensic artist uses more than drawing skills to develop a composite of a suspect. A well-trained forensic artist is also skilled at interviewing an often-traumatized witness, pulling out details and calming the person so that memories surface intact.

The key factor is the witness. How clearly did the witness see the suspect? How well can he or she remember what was seen? Was the area well lit or hidden in shadows? Was the witness traumatized in any way, and if so, does the witness suffer from post-traumatic stress? Witnesses are always apprehensive about doing composites, because they're so concerned they might make a mistake and the wrong person will be convicted based on their testimony.

The artist has to explain the process involved to create a composite so that

Deputy Chief J. Michael Deal, forensic artist

Thinking he wanted to become an artist, J. Michael Deal went to art school to study advertising design. But life being the way it is, he eventually found himself working in law enforcement, relegating his artwork to hobby status.

"The opportunity came to do composite drawings of suspects," he recalls. Soon he was off taking training at a variety of schools, and began offering his skills for free—just for the experience. Before long, he was working for several different agencies in the area.

The schools taught him how to interview suspects to get the most out of their memory. "The interview is the most important skill," he says. "You've got to have artistic skills, but the quality of the drawing is not nearly as important. You could be the best artist in the world, but if you can't get accurate, detailed information from the witness the drawing won't be good."

Today, Deal is deputy chief at the Altamonte Springs police department in Altamonte Springs, Florida—a job that keeps him plenty busy. Occasionally, however, he still finds time to do a composite. "I'd like to see more police departments hire more full-time forensic artists," he says. Aspiring forensic artists should offer their services for free to local police agencies, he suggests. "Let them see what you can do," he says. "If you offer to work for free at first, they'll use you."

"Forensic art can be a very important tool and can help solve crimes. Plus, it's a good PR tool, so that the public realizes we're doing everything we can to solve crimes."

the witness understands the artist doesn't expect a portrait. The artist points out that recall is far more difficult than recognition, which is why forensic artists use visual aids. During the interview, the witness is assured that the pressure is on the artist to do a good drawing, not on the witness to come up with the likeness.

Most forensic artists start out working in law enforcement themselves, either as police officers or crime scene specialists, administrative assistants, secretaries, and so on. Having a background in law enforcement usually makes it easier to get that first job as a forensic artist.

If you think you'd like to explore forensic art as a career, it's a good idea to take some basic classes in composite art, because these courses emphasize interview training in addition to artistic skill. College courses or art school experience is helpful, since the better you are at drawing portraits the better your

composite will be. Training in forensic art is available at several locations; one of the most famous places you can be trained is the FBI academy in Quantico, Virginia, but you must already be a police officer to be admitted. Scottsdale Art School in Scottsdale, Arizona, also offers basic and advanced courses in forensic art, and many other community colleges offer occasional classes around the country.

Once you're trained, some forensic artists go on to be certified by the International Association for Identification (IAI). For certification, an artist must have a minimum of 40 hours of education in the field of composite art from an approved school recognized by the IAI, at least one year of full-time experience, and at least 25 completed hand-drawn composites. Forensic art certification includes applications of composite drawing, facial reconstruction, age progression/child updates, and court exhibits/graphic demonstrative evidence. The Forensic Art Certification Board verifies that certified professionals meet specified qualifications.

Pitfalls

Like many jobs in law enforcement, the forensic artist is on call 24 hours a day, seven days a week—and that's once you're accepted. The hardest part of this profession is getting your foot in the door.

Perks

It can be enormously rewarding to play a part in helping to get the "bad guys," and police professionals who are also talented in art enjoy being able to combine these two jobs.

Get a Jump on the Job

If you've got a hankering to put pencil to paper to help use your artistic skills to catch criminals, you might try sitting in on a session with a forensic artist. Find a forensic artist nearby, and see if you can watch. There aren't a lot of full-time jobs at first for this skill; you've first got to establish a reputation with your local police before they'll accept you. Many experienced forensic artists recommend that you offer your services for free at first; once you've got experience and the police know your work, you can start charging.

FURNITURE MAKER

OVERVIEW

Furniture makers plan the appearance of sofas, chairs, tables, desks, bookcases, and a variety of other furniture pieces. In doing so, they must consider the latest trends in furniture, production costs, and suitable materials. Additionally, they must create furniture that is visually pleasing as well as functional.

Furniture makers who work for themselves, designing by commission, must split their time between working in the shop and drumming up business. When starting out, it can help to appear at juried art shows and furniture exhibitions, showing off the furniture to prospective customers.

The creation of a beautiful piece of wood furniture begins long before a saw meets the wood. For furniture commissioned by the customer, it begins with the artist's sketch of what the finished piece will look like, in conjunction with what the customer would like.

Just as important as the design—maybe even more so—is the type of wood that will be used to create the piece. Because wood is a natural material, there is great diversity in the quality of wood species. The most beautifully figured grades are hard to come by, difficult to work, and require such care in their match-up with adjacent boards that many furniture manufacturers actually choose to avoid them. However, to a studio furniture maker, exquisite

AT A GLANCE

Salary Range
$30,000 to $45,000 a year.

Education/Experience
Experience in both design and carpentry; an understanding of how furniture fits together.

Personal Attributes
Patience and attention to detail.

Requirements
None.

Outlook
This is an incredibly competitive field filled with woodworkers who create their own independent designs as well as those who create reproductions in an assembly-line style of manufacturing.

dramatically figured wood is the material of choice.

Once the design and wood have been chosen, the designer must have a shop large enough to accommodate the process. A modern shop with a variety of power saws and tools is almost a necessity.

Pitfalls

Paperwork is the down side to many creative businesses, according to the artists who find the details of owning a business to be drudgery. Keeping track of orders, supplies, and expenses and tax forms keep furniture makers out of their studios.

Perks

Designing furniture isn't so much work as a way of life, and to these artists it's a deeply fulfilling way to earn a living.

J.D. Lohr, furniture maker

Jeffrey Lohr is a furniture maker, woodworker, and teacher who has spent the past 28 years transmuting trees into art. For the last 15 years he's focused on creating original Arts and Crafts style designs using beautiful, one-of-a-kind woods he personally selects. "I do not and will not make reproductions of others' work," he says. Instead, Lohr chooses to create only original and limited edition pieces of his own creation. "I'm very fortunate," he says humbly. "This is a wonderful way to make a living."

With the assistance of two apprentices, he personally makes everything that bears his name. The upholstery and leaded glasswork are done by two fellow master craftsmen who work directly with him on specific projects. "I take the interesting design elements from turn-of-the-century Arts and Crafts furniture and give it my own twist," he says. "I don't go in 18 different directions. I have a style, and I don't deviate. I'm pretty much the product of an exceptional high school wood shop program of the 1960s and a strong work ethic," he says. Lohr earned a B.S. in industrial arts from Millersville State College, followed by postgraduate fine art course work at West Chester State. Although he describes himself as a jack-of-all-trades, finding interest in a wide variety of materials and processes, he says he's a master of one—woodworking.

Since his studio is just a few yards from his house, he can literally roll out of bed and right into his shop, where he spends 60 hours a week crafting his furniture. "I like what I do, so I don't see it as something to escape," he explains. "If you have to work your whole life, you might as well do what you like. I wouldn't like to be chained to a job, so dependent on it that your life revolves around a paycheck. It's very important to be proud of what you do."

Lohr recommends that potential furniture crafters be honest with themselves and identify their skills. "If you're not ambitious, woodworking is not for you," he warns. "It's something a lot of people want to do, but the competition is fierce."

A born teacher as well as woodsman, Lohr enjoys teaching but can't bring himself to stop crafting furniture long enough to teach more regularly.

"I don't remember not working in wood," he says. So important is the look of an individual log that he recently bought one huge old log and imported it from Britain to turn into furniture for a client. Trees are a lot like people, he says. Those that have lived through adversity develop much more interesting appearance. For example, a tree's efforts to fight off a fungus invading its bark will result in interesting figures within the wood. "Just like people," he says, "when we rise to a challenge, we become more interesting. I'm very happy with my life," he says. "My name means something to me on the furniture. I'm not looking for fame, but I won't let anything out the door without being 100 percent satisfied."

Get a Jump on the Job

Today's high schools rarely offer wood shop classes anymore, but if your school does, take the course. Get as much experience in safe woodworking skills as you can, and check into an apprenticeship with a furniture maker you respect.

GLASSBLOWER

OVERVIEW

You may have seen them at work in historical restoration sites or Renaissance fairs, blowing glass at the end of a long pole much like you'd blow a big bubble of gum from a pipe. Glassblowing is an old art form in which an object is created by inflating a glob of heated glass gathered on the end of a hollow iron tube or blowpipe. All that it takes to make glass is a little sand, soda and lime, and a lot of heat. Glassblowers produce quality tableware such as decanters, goblets, vases, and scientific glassware used in laboratories. Legend has it that Roman seamen, getting ready to prepare their evening meal on a beach, set their pots on top of stones made of a soda used for embalming the dead. As the fire heated both the stones and sand below, a strange liquid began to flow—and voila! Glass was born.

To make the glass, you pour the ingredients into a fireproof clay pot called a crucible. The mixture is heated for several hours in the furnace until it is ready to use. The furnace is heated to about 2,000 degrees Fahrenheit, and the glassblower keeps the glass in the furnace until it's time to move a gather of glass onto the blowpipe.

At that point, things get exciting: With the glob of glass at the tip, the glassblower carefully blows a small amount of air into the pipe to expand the glass. At the same time they spin the pipe round and swing it backwards and forwards. At this point they may pass the pipe on to an experienced glassblower

known as a finisher, who rolls the glass round on the end of the blowing iron. Next, the hot glass is rolled across a table to shape it into an object; a rim is formed with forceps. If the glass gets too cool, the glassblower can reheat it in the furnace.

After the object is finished, the glass is annealed in a long oven heated to about 800 degrees Fahrenheit; annealing prevents the glass from cracking.

The same process is used in scientific glassblowing or bench glassblowing to make the often complicated pieces of equipment used in laboratory experiments.

Glassblowers working in a factory producing tableware usually work a five-day, 39-hour week, while scientific glassblowers work a 35-hour week.

Ralph Behrendt, glassblower

Ralph Behrendt had spent 16 years in production management and sales when he decided to make a life change and turn his life over to the arts. "My love for the arts had always been a strong one," he says. He worked in photography during the 1960s and 1970s, but he wanted to incorporate his love of art with production management into one neat package—so he started a custom picture framing business. He was perfectly happy doing his own artistic framing when in 1989 he accepted a collection of art glass to sell in his gallery (Gallery B in Toledo), and after meeting well-known glass artist H. Jim Yarrito, Behrendt was hooked—he wanted to become a glassblower.

"From that day, I knew that I had to learn how to make glass," he says. "I wish I would have found it sooner! It became an obsession." After studying glassblowing at the Toledo Museum of Art, he started blowing his own glass, and he's been exhibiting his work since 1993 at art shows all across the country—about 25 different shows a year. What he loves about glassblowing is the immediacy of the craft. "It's instant gratification," he says. "Once it's done, it's done. When you put it in the oven, you're pretty sure that if you were happy with it going in, you'll be happy with it coming out."

Behrendt creates both hand-blown and hot-formed sculpture. While all of his art glass is hand-formed, hand blown requires blowing a bubble into the molten material. These forms become vessels such as bowls, vases, plates and art lamps. The solid sculptural forms are created in much the same way, but without using air. "The blown shapes I choose to create have flowing lines as if they were awash in the sea," he explains. "While my bowl forms are very free form, they all evolve from a very precise shape."

His sculptural forms are also created with a feeling of the sea. He creates shell forms resembling a chambered nautilus by building up layer upon layer of hot molten glass while adding elements of color in between. After the shell has been properly cooled slowly in an oven, the glass form is cut in a diamond saw to reveal its face. Once cut, it is then ground and polished with a careful hand.

While he loves his work, he cautions young artists that it can be difficult these days to open up a glassblowing studio. "Things have changed in last five years," he says. "It's gotten so expensive to do this. Natural gas prices have gone through roof." It's a serious financial commitment, because once you flip that switch on the gas line, he says, you start burning gas. His furnace runs constantly about 11 months of year straight, because the oven is so temperature-sensitive it's risky to turn it off and on.

Nevertheless, it's an art form he loves—and he'd never go back to the corporate world. Behrendt describes his glassblowing as "art in the moment." It can an intense, time-consuming thing to create glass. "Taking a break in the middle of the session is impossible," he says. "There must be a feel for the piece being created, and timing is crucial," he says. Too cold and the creation can crack and fall off the pipe—too hot and it goes out of control. "A relationship is established with each piece of art glass," he says, "which requires the patience and tenderness of a loved one. The result is one of exquisite beauty."

Pitfalls

Conditions can be hot and noisy, and burns are possible.

Perks

Blowing glass is a difficult, challenging, but creatively exciting job that can be artistically satisfying.

Get a Jump on the Job

The best way to learn about glassblowing is to get books from the library and see if you can work as an apprentice or intern with an established glassblower.

GRAVESTONE CARVER

OVERVIEW

A stone carver who works in the historical manner uses a chisel and mallet to incise inscriptions and designs into stone, most often slate, chosen for its beauty and long-lasting quality. Carvers may use slate quarried in different parts of the country (red, purple, green, or black, depending on the part of the country). Some artists import their slate from Wales, which has blue-black slate of superior quality. Although marble is a beautiful stone, it deteriorates in the weather and will crumble after about 100 years.

Once a gravestone carver has chosen the slate, he or she must meet with the family to decide on the wording, the style, and the design. Once these decisions have been made, the artist typically begins by creating a scale drawing. After the slate slab is cut at the quarry to the correct size, the inscription is laid out on the stone.

Now the carving can begin: The carver dips a chisel in a bucket of water and drags it across a sharpening stone, because to produce the hairline beginnings of a letter, the chisel has to be sharp. Painstakingly, the chisel and mallet are manipulated carefully to incise the letters into the stone.

It can take from a few days for a small inscription to many weeks to finish a gravestone by hand.

Pitfalls

The work can be tedious, and the paper-work required to maintain a business,

frustrating. Carving gravestones can be emotionally distressing, because carvers must work with grieving families.

Perks

To an artist who loves to work in stone, carving gravestones the old-fashioned way can be a gloriously freeing, creative way to make a living. Many carvers also enjoy knowing their artwork will stand for hundreds of years, giving pleasure to grieving families and those who appreciate the beauty of stone carving.

Get a Jump on the Job

If you love letters and carving, you can start by practicing to carve in wood. If you can find a carver nearby, see if you can act as an apprentice. Read lots of books about historical stone carvers and keep on practicing!

Karin Sprague, gravestone carver

At a little cottage in the Rhode Island woods, lamplight burns late into the night as carver Karin Sprague patiently works on the inscription for a slate marker she's designed to honor a beloved family member. "I feel this is the work I've been called to do," Sprague says. "There is a ministry to this."

Sprague is one of only a dozen artisans in the United States who practices the ancient art of 18th century gravestone carving, and she's welcomed into her studio a select handful of other carvers, several of whom have acted as her apprentice in the past.

The soft-spoken stone carver was born with a love of letters. As a child, she'd cut out interesting letters and logos and post them on her bedroom wall. "Letters spoke to me then," she remembers. "I just loved to look at them." Encouraged by a high school art teacher to study photography, she attended Paier College of Art in Hamden, Connecticut. "But photography didn't feed me," she says, and she moved on to practice wood-carving, working at a sign shop in East Greenwich, Rhode Island.

Driving through the rural areas in the northwest corner of the state, she would often pull over and walk into the woods, examining the lettering on old gravestones. "Carving letters in stone would be the ultimate," she thought to herself. When she finally got a chance to put mallet to stone, the first three letters she decided to carve were: G.O.D. As she was carving the "G," she suddenly realized she had found her life's work. "This is it!" she thought. "It was so powerful—so right." The first gravestone she carved was for her husband's father. "It was done as an incredible act of love," she remembers. Soon after that, she began carving gravestones for others as well.

She draws her own designs and letters, and—together with the four others in her shop—each stone is carved by hand. It is meticulous, painstaking work, yet fundamentally creative and intimate. "There is that flourish the hand can give at the beginning or the end of a letter, and there's beauty in that," she says.

Karin carves each stone according to the unique wishes of her clients. In the beginning, she sits down with each one to listen to the story of the life of the one she will honor in stone. It can be difficult, but it's an important part of the process. "I have the thrill of doing what I love," she says. "Slowly working with the families. Not everyone understands, but many families know that this is a ministry for me that I'm called to do." Families appreciate the gentleness and caring with which she discusses the stone. "They send me letters telling me how the experience really helped them," she says.

For example, she carved one stone for a young boy to honor his belief in time travel. Sprague created an upright slate stone pierced by an arch, which functions as an arched doorway in the center, allowing light to flow through it. The boy's mother decided she wanted to have her stone set flush with the earth on the other side of his stone, so that at the day and hour of his birth, the sun would shine through his arch, and rake right across her name.

Her advice to budding carvers? "Follow your bliss," she says. "Whatever you do, make sure it is something you love. Make sure that what you do is something that makes you sing."

Now an established stone carver, Sprague is kept busy creating lasting memorials and other works for clients across the United States. She and her fellow carvers can produce about 30 stones a year, and at the moment she has more than a full year's worth of work waiting to be done, since each piece can take months to create.

"There is a story in words, the shape of the stone. So many gravestones today have nothing besides a name and a date. There is no soul in the stone, no hand. To me, carving in stone is overwhelmingly beautiful."

GREETING CARD WRITER

OVERVIEW

Have you ever stood in a gift shop sifting through hundreds of greeting cards, and thought to yourself: "Hey! I could write this!" There are quite a few people who do, both as freelance greeting card writers and those working for large card corporations as in-house scribes. And there's an ever-growing market for cards: Americans buy almost 7 billion cards a year, and just three companies control 85 percent of the market: Hallmark, American Greetings, and Gibson Greetings. However, besides these Big Three, there are about 3,000 other greeting card publishers in the United States—so there's plenty of opportunity out there! And since more than 90 percent of all U.S. households buy greeting cards and the average person gets more than 20 a year, there's an endless hunger for your work.

The exchange of greeting cards is one of the most widely accepted customs in the United States, and there are cards for virtually any occasion or relationship. About 100,000 retail outlets around the country carry greeting cards, where women buy more than 80 percent of all cards. Although women are more likely than men to buy several cards at once, men generally spend more on a single card than women.

Most greeting card writers freelance, because most greeting card companies don't keep a large stable of greeting card writers on staff. However, the largest companies, including Hallmark, prefer to

AT A GLANCE

Salary Range
Freelance fees: $25 to $150 per card.

Education/Experience
High school diploma; college not required, but writing courses or journalism degree might be helpful.

Personal Attributes
Should be keen observers of society and the environment, excellent verbal communicators, creative, innovative, artistic, and curious.

Requirements
Ability to write and a keen sense of universal themes.

Outlook
Good to excellent, both for freelance writers and corporate employees (if you're willing to relocate).

maintain a large number of writers and refuse all freelance requests.

But whether you work for yourself or for someone else, the job of crafting greeting cards is pretty much the same: You don't write what you want to say, but what the consumer wants to say. The ability to capture exactly what that consumer wants to say—but doesn't know how—is the key to a successful career as a card author. As a result, greeting card writers must combine basic writing flair, considerable sensitivity and "heart," plus an understanding of what's on consumers' minds, so they can write messages for cards that help people connect with one another.

There are just about as many styles of greeting cards as there are consumers to buy them: traditional, rhymed verse, funny, ironic, off-color, sweet, poetry. Basically, however, there are two categories of greeting cards—*seasonal* and *everyday*. The most popular everyday cards are birthday, anniversary, get well, friendship, and sympathy cards. The most popular seasonal cards are Christmas, Valentine's Day, Mother's Day, Easter, and Father's Day cards.

Each company has different card *lines* that feature one of these styles. If you're working as a freelance greeting card writer, you'll need to decide which style fits you best, and then find the company to whom you want to send your ideas. First, you'll need to go to a card store and inspect the cards, writing down the publisher's name and some sample lines. Companies that accept freelance submissions have their own guidelines, which you'll need to follow precisely. (Most card companies have Web sites that detail their guidelines; you can also find these guidelines in the current year's *Writer's Market*.) Typically, you'll need to write your ideas on index cards (some companies want separate index cards; others will accept a sheet of paper with a list of ideas), usually in batches of 10. A few companies are beginning to warm up to the idea of e-mail ideas, but most still like to see a paper copy the old fashioned way—sent through the mail. Once you mail them off (including a self-addressed, stamped envelope, of course) you can wait a few weeks to a few months to hear whether any of your ideas are accepted.

Several of the largest card companies, such as American Greetings and Hallmark, don't accept unsolicited submissions. If you decide that greeting cards is something you'd like to try full-time as a paid staffer, you'll want to try to land a job writing cards for these giant companies. Each of these companies' Web sites contains job pages that you can monitor to see if there are openings.

And now a word about electronic cards: At the moment, most greeting cards are sent the old-fashioned way, but someday e-cards could have a significant impact on the greeting card industry and shift some of the opportunities for writers from the standard print format to electronic cards. Although card companies may have initially been worried about what electronic communication would do to card sales, in fact things have never been better. E-mail and other electronic methods of communicating have given Americans a convenient and inexpensive way to keep in contact with friends and acquaintances, and the increased use of electronic communication seems to be boosting rather than reducing sales of traditional greeting cards. Some sociologists believe this is because the Internet has allowed people to increase the number of relationships they are able to maintain, which then prompts them to send cards the traditional way.

Pitfalls

Competition as a freelance greeting card writer can be fierce, and it's an insecure sort of way to make a living, since you never know how many card ideas will sell at any point. It can also be lonely, penning verses in your office all by yourself.

Perks

The flip side of insecurity is freedom, and freelance greeting card writers have lots of freedom—to write the kinds of messages they want, when and how they want, and to work as much or as little as they like. Staff writers find that the very large card companies are very employee-friendly, creative places to work that combine good salaries, lots of support, with a creative and fun job. No matter how you write your verses, there is a lot of personal satisfaction

Molly Wigand, Hallmark greeting card writer

As a high school newspaper reporter, Molly Wigand thought the best job in the world would be a greeting card writer—but she never dreamed she'd ever get the chance to land such a job! After earning a B.A. in news-editorial journalism from the University of Minnesota, she answered a blind ad in 1979 and the next thing she knew, she was working at Hallmark. Three years later, she met her husband—also a writer—and then left Hallmark to raise their three sons. During this time, she wrote children's books featuring the Rugrats and Scooby Doo, and completed *How to Write and Sell Greeting Cards, Bumper Stickers, T-Shirts and Other Fun Stuff* (see Read More About It at the end of this book).

She was only too happy to return to Hallmark full time in 1999. The legendary family-friendly Hallmark environment makes going to work fun, Wigand says: "I have two families—one at home, and one at work."

After more than two decades at Hallmark, Molly has gained a reputation for writing earthy, from-the-heart, reality-based husband-and-wife cards. Her job varies from day to day, depending on what stack of projects comes across her desk. "At the moment, we're focusing on kids projects, with cards that pop up and slide, creating motion," she says. "Other times, I might get a request for Valentine cards for a specific group of consumers."

No matter what the requests may be for a particular type of card, however, the underlying theme is caring, honesty, and connection. "It really is about playing a role and figuring out what a person would want to say," she explains. Once she comes up with copy, it goes to an editorial committee for approval. "For humorous copy, two out of 10 of my ideas might get approved on a good day," she says. "My longer prose and verse, I have a higher acceptance rate."

There's not much chance of being bored, since Wigand can write not just cards but packaging for ornaments, plates, plaques—all sorts of products that require heartfelt sentiments. "As far as I can tell," she says, "it's the most purely creative job a writer can have in a corporate environment." Wigand suggests that would-be greeting card writers should try making cards for friends and spending lots of time journaling. While getting a degree in writing or journalism can be helpful, it's not a requirement to work as a greeting card writer at Hallmark, whose staffers currently include a former drywall installer and a former nurse. "While verbal training is helpful," Wigand says, "the most important quality, whether you're writing serious or humorous cards, is that the person is in touch with the way people are to each other. What's important is what's in your heart."

in knowing your work is brightening the lives of others.

Get a Jump on the Job

Hallmark offers college juniors a summer internship program (go to http://www.hallmark.com, click on *careers* and then *summer internships*) at the Hallmark headquarters in Kansas City, Missouri. If you're interested in a greeting card career, why not try some submissions on your own? Check out the online versions of *Writers Market* for a list greeting card markets.

HOLOGRAPHER

OVERVIEW

There she was, the shimmery, shining vision of Princess Leia, whispering "Obi-Wan!" over and over in the first *Star Wars* movie. For many people, that was the first depiction of a hologram they'd ever seen.

Holography is a technique that allows the recording and playback of true, three-dimensional images. A hologram is often described as a three-dimensional picture. Although this is a good way to get a general idea of what you'd experience looking at one, holograms have very little in common with traditional photography. While a photograph has an actual physical image, a hologram contains information about the size, shape, brightness, and contrast of the object being recorded. This information is stored in a microscopic complex pattern made possible by the properties of light generated by a laser.

Holograms provide what is called *parallax*, which allows the viewer to move back and forth, up and down, and see different perspectives—as if the object were actually there. If you took a regular picture of a big marble, and there was a smaller marble behind it, you wouldn't be able to look around the big marble to see the little one. With a hologram, you can look around the big marble and see the little one behind it, because a hologram is in three dimensions.

Looking at a hologram is just like looking at something that's real, right in front of you. Some holograms are so real that you want to take your hand and touch the object in it—but your hand would go right through thin air. In fact, all of those really cool special effects you love in movies today will one day seem incredibly outdated. In the future, it will be possible to receive 3-D holographic images right in your home, and you'll see the action as if it was taking place right in your own living room.

An artist can create a hologram to test all kinds of things—everything from car engines to aircraft tires. Holograms can be used in medical imaging, so that doctors can take measurements within the holographic image. Simple, colorful holograms are used on consumer packaging materials and credit cards. Pilots use holographic optical elements (HOEs) to help them keep their eyes on the sky or the runway while still being able to read their instrumentation, which appears to float in front of their cockpit window. This feature is already available as an option on several cars as well.

Sharon McCormack, holographer

Sharon McCormack was born in New York City and now lives and works in the Columbia River Gorge National Scenic Area in White Salmon, Washington. Since 1975, she has been owner and director of the School of Holography in San Francisco.

As a self-described "art-oholic," she loved art from the beginning—long before discovering holography. Eventually, she found that no other medium gave her the satisfaction of this high-tech art form.

She spends her time working on hologram exhibits, commissioned work, and holography consulting. Her largest exhibit is dedicated to the tradition of American Native tribes, including many 180° and 360° animated stereograms (a type of hologram).

McCormack has created many group and solo exhibitions around the world, winning awards and grants, and her work has been featured on the covers of *Sports Illustrated, National Geographic,* and Prince's CD *Diamonds and Pearls.*

"If picture is worth a thousand words," she says, "a hologram is worth a million."

Holographic lenses and contacts can make one lens provide several different functions, such as correcting regular vision while acting as a magnifier for reading—all in the same lens, and throughout the entire lens at the same time. Holograms can be made into portraits of people and pets, and artists use holography to express their creativity. They also can be used on magazine and book covers, for advertising, and for data storage such as holographic hard drives. In fact, the entire contents of the Library of Congress can be stored in the area the size of a sugar cube!

Holography was invented by Dr. Dennis Gabor at the Imperial College of London as a result of his attempts to improve the resolution of the scanning electron microscope; in 1971 he received the Nobel Prize in physics for his invention. To this day, holography continues to provide the most accurate depiction of three-dimensional images in the world.

Holographers work in professional holography labs, producing the holograms that you see in stores, galleries, and other places. A typical lab consists of a laser, lenses, mirrors, optical holders, and other assorted equipment, plus a darkroom for processing the hologram.

There are many types of holograms and hologram artists. Artists create holographic portraits, poems, drawings, architectural glass, environments, stage sets, primitive movies, narratives, large format outdoor works, public art commissions, room installations, wet-and-dry holograms, etched and scratched holograms, sun-lit holograms, architectural holography, and holography combined with mixed media, slides, or video.

As a holographic artist, you'll work with many different kinds of holographic images. Some artists make most of their salary creating art commissions; these lucky artists are free to create exactly the kind of holographic images they wish. Their work is typically displayed in galleries or sold for private enjoyment and display. Most holographic artists also do commercial work for a wide variety of clients, including hospitals and physicians, stores, businesses, ad agencies, and movie companies. Artists may help produce holograms used on magazine covers.

Pitfalls

The equipment needed to produce this type of modern technology can be expensive; only certain individuals are open to buying this type of art form.

Perks

Techno-artists and those who love new, edgy forms of art can truly experience all sorts of innovative ways to be creative.

Get a Jump on the Job

The best way to learn more about this type of career would be to find a holographer and volunteer or apprentice in the shop to learn if this art form might be something you'd like to focus on.

JEWELRY DESIGNER

OVERVIEW

Gold and silver rings, earrings, pendants, necklaces—no matter what the piece, a jeweler or goldsmith is behind its design, creation, and repair. Some artists design expensive, high-end jewelry using only the most precious metals and gems. These are the folks who set diamonds and rubies into gold and platinum settings, crafting pieces that sell for hundreds of thousands of dollars in exclusive jewelry stores and galleries. Others design and craft lower-priced jewelry using materials like silver and turquoise, selling at craft shows, art galleries, and in small shops.

Although gold and silver are typically used for jewelry, you can actually use a wide variety of substances for your designs, including metal, plastic, ceramic, and wood. They also use many varied techniques. Some jewelry is set with stones; some is hand-painted. Some is heavy and solid; some is fine and delicate. As a result, the skills and knowledge that jewelry making requires also varies widely and can include mold making, casting, soldering, polishing, gem-cutting, setting, and much more. Many jewelry makers specialize in just one or two of these things. Others spend most of their time repairing broken clasps, resetting stones, and resizing wedding rings.

While it may seem pleasant to sit around all day crafting jewels and lumps of gold into art, if you're self-employed—and a third of all jewelers

are—the business can be extremely stressful, especially around the December holidays. You've also got to know how to run a business and attract sales, which means knowing how to advertise and market your work, keep the books, and take care of taxes.

As technology continues to march forward, you've also got to be comfortable

AT A GLANCE

Salary Range

Entry-level workers earn $18,000 to $25,000; experienced jewelers and goldsmiths can surpass $60,000. Salaries vary depending on employer and location. Many earn a commission for each piece of jewelry sold on top of a base salary.

Education/Experience

Career diploma or certificate; programs are offered at art schools in universities, or in jewelry schools.

Personal Attributes

Artistic sense, a steady hand, precision, creativity, ability to work well with customers, patience, good eyesight, and a flair for design.

Requirements

Jewelers of America offers four levels of professional certification for jewelry makers, ranging from Certified Bench Jeweler Technician to Certified Master Bench Jeweler. Candidates must pass both written and practical exams to become certified. Certification may be helpful in finding a job, since some employers prefer to hire certified jewelry makers.

Outlook

There's a shortage of highly skilled, well-trained jewelers and goldsmiths, which is expected to continue as older artists retire. Job opportunities should be good, especially for graduates of jewelry maker training programs.

Dan Sessa, jewelry designer

Methuen, Massachusetts, designer Dan Sessa has been working with jewelry ever since he was 13 years old, when he helped his dad with the family jewelry business. Six years later, as his father lay critically ill in bed at home, young Dan began doing more and more of the work, checking with his dad whenever he had questions. "When he passed away, I realized this was the only thing I'd ever done, so at 21, I took over the business." A few stores didn't think the young Sessa would be capable of handling the business, and dropped him; over the years, most of those stores have returned.

As a young goldsmith, Sessa spent a lot of his time designing jewelry for family members—especially his wife, whom he met when he was 16 and she was 15. Today, almost all of his business is in designing gold pieces, although about 30 percent of his work is in platinum. Although he's also a silversmith, he finds the characteristics of silver more difficult to work with.

For those not so fortunate to have a father who's a jeweler, the best way to learn the craft is by attending a jeweler's school, Sessa says. "It's a very difficult field to learn on your own," he explains. "It's great to have someone actually show you how to solder, how the different temperatures affect what you're doing. I watched my father constantly."

Sessa teaches a few classes, and he says he'd like to do more, but the pressures of his clients give him little time to devote to classes. In addition to creating individual pieces for private clients, Sessa also maintains a number of stores, which he will visit and work on the premises. "The stress level is very high," he says, "and I've got to do eight hours of work in two hours." Occasionally, he'll also visit a gem show and sell his pieces.

Sessa is a master repairer, but repairs are far less exciting than designing and making pieces. "I can do a ring in an hour or a day, depending on the complexity," he says, although some projects can take up to 100 hours. Working out of his home, he typically spends 12 hours a day at his bench, although he says he tries to slow down in the summers. Starting with November, he works about 100 hours a week, straight through until August.

So will he bring any of his children into the business? "I'd rather they go to college," he says. "They see the stress level of this job, and it's just not worth it for the amount of money you make."

Still, he says he loves the work and the creative satisfaction of designing just the right ring or brooch for his clients. "You can get into a rhythm when you're working. I really love it."

using new technology, such as lasers to cut stones, engrave, and weld. Some jewelers use computer-aided design (CAD) programs like Matrix or Jewelspace to create a *virtual reality* model of a piece where flaws show up easily in the initial stage of design.

In addition to designing jewelry, artists also make molds and pour metal, solder and polish jewelry, set gems and pearls, engrave, and manage retail jewelry businesses.

Jewelry makers may do it all, or they may specialize in a particular type or style of jewelry. Some make chains, or rings, or brooches. Others may be involved primarily in design, casting, setting stones, or any of the other processes involved in jewelry making. Some specialize in the repair and restoration of antique pieces, and others offer appraisal services.

You can learn how to create jewelry at specialized jewelry schools, or apprentice to a jeweler, learning on the job. For students who want to go into jewelry design or work in a small shop, the best route is to complete a college program in jewelry making or attend a jewelry making school. College programs, which offer formal degrees in jewelry making, are usually offered by art departments and focus on the creative aspects of jewelry making and design. College programs tend to view making jewelry as a personal art form, while jewelry schools tend to be more practical, offering courses in sales, marketing, management, and appraisal as well as jewelry making. They usually award career diplomas or certificates rather than degrees. In either case, though, new jewelry makers usually receive extensive additional on the job training after landing their first job.

Pitfalls

You can work long, tedious, stressful hours bent over your bench and earn only low to moderate salaries.

Perks

Most jewelers work in the business because they love designing, working with their hands, and they love jewels.

Get a Jump on the Job

If you love to work with jewelry, try visiting your local artist and see if you can help around the shop, or enter into a formal apprenticeship. While you can get books out of the library that illustrate the craft, you really need hands-on experience to learn how to be a gold or silversmith or jeweler.

KNITTING PATTERN DESIGNER

OVERVIEW

It's not just white-haired grandmas who are knitting and crocheting anymore, according to a study by the Craft Yarn Council of America (CYCA). More than 38 million people were knitting, purling, and crocheting in 2002, 4 million more than were knitting in 1994 survey. About 17.3 million of those knitters were under 45—and those knitters are looking for hip, trendy, unusual projects to knit. To the rescue are knitting pattern designers, who spend their time designing the patterns that knitters fall in love with in the pages of knitting books and magazines.

It's a long hard road, getting that pattern from an initial concept to print. Rejection happens, even to the best of designers. Designers need to remember that rejection isn't personal—there are any number of reasons that a pattern doesn't make the grade. Perhaps the editor just bought a similar pattern from another designer a few days before. Or maybe the swatch (a sample of knitting) sent in with the pattern was done in green, and the editor hates green, so subconsciously she never goes ahead with a sweater in green. Or it could simply be that the editor is just having a bad day. If the designer believes the pattern is a good, quality idea, he or she needs to be persistent and submit it to other publications. (The information in this entry is applicable to designing for

the craft industry in general, regardless of whether you're designing knitting patterns, plastic canvas patterns, papercraft projects, or general craft projects.)

In addition to writing good patterns, perhaps the two most important things for the pattern designer to know are the editorial calendar and the submission guidelines—both of which are available from the magazine and are sometimes listed on the magazine's Web site.

Lily Chin, knit and crochet pattern designer

Perhaps Lily Chin was destined to become a knit and crochet pattern designer. Not only did Chin learn to knit and crochet from her mother at an early age, but she grew up in New York City in the heart of the fashion industry.

Today, Chin is one of the leading knit and crochet pattern designers in the world. Her patterns have appeared in every major knitting-related magazine on the market today, as well as numerous other publications. Chin has also authored three books on the subject: *Mosaic Magic: Afghans Made Easy (Crochet Treasury)*, *The Urban Knitter*, and *Knit and Crochet with Beads*. Her designs have even been featured in the *Sports Illustrated* swimsuit issue.

"It's very specialized; there are no schools that teach it [in the United States]," says Chin, who studied art in school. "You can learn some design in art school, and you can pick up a lot from books." She likens it to an "independent study"—where you learn a lot on your own. Chin says there are more opportunities to learn today, and she encourages students to attend conferences like those offered by The Knitting Guild of America (TKGA), the Crochet Guild of America (CGOA), as well as the Stitches events (sponsored by XRX, Inc., publisher of *Knitter's Magazine*).

Not only is Chin great at what she does, but she truly enjoys it. "I'm in charge. I get to pick and choose my projects. I don't always know where my next check is coming from, but I also don't have to put on pantyhose and go into the office everyday."

Chin is very candid in her advice to pattern designer hopefuls. "It's very limited. Don't quit your day job just yet. I only know a few people (three or four) making a living at it. This business ebbs and flows: Knitting is hot now, but it won't always be!"

"It's very competitive. Lots of people are doing it because it's fun and they can do it from home, and any money they make is a plus, icing on the cake." Chin says that all the competition drives down the going price editors and magazines are willing to pay for a pattern.

But for someone who is determined to become a pattern designer and make a living at it, Chin adds that there are other things you can do in the profession to make ends meet, such as teaching, writing books, or working for the manufacturing sector on the side.

An editor might pass on a terrific Christmas stocking pattern because it lands on her desk while she's in the middle of planning the spring issue. The editorial calendar lets the designer know how far in advance patterns should be submitted.

Submission guidelines are also critical: Another pattern might get rejected because an enthusiastic designer sends only a sketch of the sweater with very brief written instructions and the editor wants to see a completed knit item and written instructions. The submission guidelines tell the designer exactly how and what to send when submitting a pattern for possible publication.

You don't need a college degree to be a knitting pattern designer, but you do need to be able to knit, and knit well. A strong background in basic math (especially fractions) is also important: You need to be able to take the information you get from knitting a swatch and use it to make all the calculations for the garment you're designing. You also need math skills so that you can write the directions for your pattern in multiple sizes.

Once the pattern is written, you'll hire a contract knitter to knit the garment. If you knit up each pattern as you designed it, you'd end up spending all your time knitting, and wouldn't get much designing done.

The Knitting Guild Association (TKGA) offers a three-level Master Knitting Program in which participants master a number of knitting techniques, plus write at least one pattern following the standard industry format. This opportunity allows you to get feedback and suggestions on your pattern, allowing you to learn from your mistakes. Many of the patterns students write as a part of the program get published in *Cast On* magazine, the official TKGA publication.

Another way to prepare to become a knitting pattern designer is to be familiar with as many of the knitting publications as possible. Each knitting magazine has its own niche. You might come up with a terrific design for a baby sweater, but if you submit it to a magazine that only publishes adult patterns, chances are very strong it'll be rejected.

Pitfalls

There are very few full-time pattern designer jobs available, which means no steady income and no paid benefits, which can be stressful. You're responsible for paying the contract knitters that you hire.

Perks

You get to work from home, working in your pajamas or at 3 a.m. if you want. It's fun to create designs and see your name in print. Once you make a name for yourself, the editors will come to you for patterns.

Get a Jump on the Job

Learn to knit if you don't already know how, and practice! Master the basic skills and techniques. Get some good basic patterns for sweaters, socks, hats, mittens, and other knit items. Study the pattern. Figure out how the basic pieces are made and then put together.

LAMPWORK BEAD ARTIST

OVERVIEW

Beads have played a role in the history of nearly every culture on earth. They haven't only been used to adorn people, but they also have been used to decorate and embellish traditional costumes. They have been used in religious objects and ceremonies. They have even been used as a form of currency. In fact, according to one version of American history, it's been said that Dutch settlers bought Manhattan Island for approximately $24 worth of beads.

Beading is a very popular hobby these days, and one of the most popular type of beads on the market are lampwork (sometimes called *flamework*) beads. The term *lampwork* refers to the oil lamps used by artisans hundreds of years ago in the making of these types of beads. To make these stunning works of art, lampwork artists work with thin rods of glass and a heat source. Some beginners start with an inexpensive propane torch, but professionals work with torches that use a mixture of oxygen and propane together. These torches burn cleaner, hotter, and have a more adjustable flame. The glass rods are melted in the flame of the torch. The molten glass is then wrapped around a stainless steel rod called a mandrel. When the mandrel is removed, it will leave a hole through the bead so that it can be strung or used some other way in a piece of jewelry.

Through trial and error, practice, and experience, lampwork artists learn the properties of different kinds of glass and how to work with it. They know how

AT A GLANCE

Salary Range

A lampwork bead can range in price from just a few dollars to $75 per bead, or more. To price their beads, most lampwork artists charge $1 to $2 per minute that it takes to make that bead. For example, if it takes five minutes, the beadmaker would sell it for $5 to $10, depending on the market. Sometimes higher-end, more in-demand beads will bring more than the $1 to $2 per minute, especially for an established artist who has made a name for him or herself.

Education/Experience

Training with an experienced lampwork artist is recommended.

Personal Attributes

Lampwork bead artists need to be safety conscious, but not afraid of getting cut or burned. They need to be detail-oriented, with a good sense of color and design. They have to be adventurous and willing to try new things. Must be able to work alone in the studio for long periods of time

Requirements

None.

Outlook

The outlook for beadmakers depends in part on the economy and trends in the fashion industry, but these should continue to be a demand for high-quality, well-made, unique beads.

much it takes for the glass to reach the point where they can work with it. They learn how much a bead can be heated until it starts to loose its shape. And they learn how to use the glass to create the effects they desire. Some artists create beads with layers of different colors. Others encase tiny glass flowers inside their beads. Some actually use the glass like a paintbrush, creating designs and textured effects on the outer surface of the glass.

After the beads are created, all professional lampwork artists *kiln-anneal* their beads. Glass shrinks as it cools. If it cools too quickly, it can crack. To prevent the beads from cracking, they are cooled in a kiln where the temperature can be regulated, and slowly reduced to room temperature.

Lampwork artists use a number of avenues to sell their beads. Some sell their beads from the studios. Others work with specialty shops and boutiques to sells their beads. Those beads might be sold outright to the specialty shop or handled on a consignment basis. Many sell their beads at bead shows or on the Internet. Many artists spend as much time marketing and selling their beads as they do making them.

There are many good videos and books on the market to teach you the basics of making lampwork beads. But books and videos are not the best way to learn all the ins and outs of lampwork beadmaking. They are, however, terrific resources for learning different tips and techniques once you have some experience making beads. The photos in many of the books are wonderful sources of inspiration.

The best way to learn the art of lampwork beadmaking is to take a class from an expert. Like many forms of glasswork, you use an open flame and pressurized fuel source when making lampwork beads. And, while there is always a danger when working with fuel and fire, it can be done safely. Training with an experienced lampwork artist is a good way to learn the safety procedures and precautions that will help to keep you from getting hurt.

Another good reason to take classes before setting up your own workshop is because it is expensive. It can cost $1,000 or more to get started, and do it right. And, if you don't have a place to set up shop, you'll have the added expense of building or renting a space. It's a much better investment to spend a few hundred dollars to make sure you enjoy the process of creating lampwork beads, before spending thousands of dollars on equipment and supplies. Some instructors actually rent equipment and/or studio time so that you can try it for a while before having to purchase your own equipment.

As a lampwork artist, you'll constantly be learning something new. You'll try new techniques you read about in books, magazines, and online, and you'll develop tricks and techniques of your own as you work to create unique, innovative new beads.

Pitfalls

With the popularity of lampwork beads, many people have taken to making and selling beads. To make a living, you'll have to work hard at marketing your work, and you can't count on a steady paycheck from week to week.

Perks

Your beads may become part of a piece of jewelry that is passed down from generation to generation, becoming a family heirloom. You can set your own hours, which is especially nice when you have young children at home.

Get a Jump on the Job

Read through the books and watch the videos that are available so that you are familiar with the terminology and basic process of how lampwork beads are created. Look for lampwork beadmaking classes and workshops in your area. While

Leslie Videki, glass artist

Glass artist Leslie Videki got her start by making jewelry using other people's beads. A trip to visit a friend in Arizona changed all that. "My friend had just gotten into lampwork and fusing [another type of hot glass art]. I tried it, and I knew that I wanted to do it." Once Videki saved enough money to get started, she loaded her two small sons and large chocolate lab into the car and drove 100 miles to buy a kiln. She started making fused glass pieces and selling them on eBay.

It was necessity that turned her hobby into her career. "I split up with my husband. He lost his job, so I knew I wouldn't get much support from him. Then 9/11 happened." With no money coming home, the stay-at-home mom looked for a job, with no luck. "My mom and my sister encouraged me to try it [turning glass art into a full-time career]. My sister loaned me the money to get a bigger kiln." Videki started turning out fused pieces. She was doing two firings a day, and she had anywhere from 20 to 50 pieces listed on eBay at any given time.

That year, her mom gave her a lampwork bead kit as an early Christmas present, and soon after she took her first class. A year and a half later, Videki had a studio of her own and started teaching classes. Today, Videki spends her days in her studio teaching and making mostly lampwork beads, so she doesn't do as much fusing as she once did. She sells her work in shops, on the Internet, and at some of the biggest bead shows around the country. (To see some of Videki's beads, check out http://www.bead-goddess.com.)

As for the future of lampwork beads, Videki thinks, "There will be a shift to beads for jewelry to beads as collectible or artistic items," adding, "There will always be a demand for quality beads for jewelry."

For students hoping to follow in her footsteps, she jokes that you need to have a rich husband (or wife). On a more serious note, she says, "It's a struggle, and it's not easy. I probably wouldn't recommend it as a sole source of income."

some instructors might not accept students under 18 years old, because of liability issues, others will. Technically, if anything happens to a student while he or she is making lampwork beads, the instructor is liable.

LOGO DESIGNER

OVERVIEW

Think for a moment about all the companies or products that are recognized around the world from a simple graphic image: the Chevy bowtie, McDonald's golden arches, the Gerber baby, the Nike swoosh, the Pillsbury doughboy, and the NBC peacock. You can probably name dozens if not hundreds of other companies that you'd recognize from the logo alone.

In fact, it seems nowadays everyone has a logo: sports teams, universities, clubs and organizations, churches, restaurants, and shopping malls. And logos aren't just for large corporations—think about all the small businesses in your hometown that have a logo that they use in advertising and on promotional items.

In this global economy, with easy access to information and products from every corner of the globe, a distinctive and easily recognizable, established logo is one way of bridging the gaps in communication and understanding. But logos aren't a new thing—actually, they've been around for a long, long time. Logos date as far back as ancient Greece. Early logos began as a cipher made from a single letter. Eventually these ciphers evolved into a design or mark with two or more intertwined letters. These early logos were used on things such as stationary and business cards.

Over the centuries, the rudimentary logos developed into the mason's marks, gold and silversmiths' marks, and papermaker's watermarks that the craftsmen used to distinguish their work.

AT A GLANCE

Salary Range

$30,000 to $45,000, depending on experience and education.

Education/Experience

Degree in graphic design, marketing, advertising, or related field; or comparable on-the-job experience.

Personal Attributes

Artistic and creative. Able to work quickly and professionally under pressure. Able to meet tight deadlines. Willing to rework a project as needed to meet the specifications of the client. Good people skills and communication skills are very important. Technology-literate with good computer skills.

Requirements

None.

Outlook

With new businesses springing up every day, more and more companies are seeking to stand out among their competitors in an increasingly global economy. As a result, the outlook for logo designers is expected to be strong. However, there is often a lot of competition for job openings.

Publishers and printers also developed marks to identify their work. Logos are used in much the same way today, to help consumers identify products and company brands while protecting against "knock-offs."

It's the job of the logo designer to develop the graphic image that will be used on items to help identify the product, brand, and company. Once a client hires your company to design a logo, the process begins by finding out more about the client's business and what he has in mind for a logo. That information might be collected by a face-to-face meeting, over the phone, or nowadays, more often than not, over the Internet via e-mail or a Web survey. Then the logo designer begins working up several different designs. Depending on the level of service the customer has chosen, there may be several different designers all assigned to the same job, giving the client more variety from which to choose.

Some logo design companies offer very quick turnaround time, some as little as 60 minutes. That means the logo designers must be able to develop several ideas very quickly to meet that deadline. Other companies may spend 10 days or more designing the initial logo ideas.

After the initial logo designs are delivered to the client, he'll choose the one that he likes best. The client is usually given the option to make changes to that logo. Again, the number of changes and revisions or refinements is usually based on the level of service purchased.

Once the client is happy with the logo, the finished design is usually saved in a wide variety of formats so that it can be used however the client needs.

If helping a company to define its visual image by designing unique and innovative logos sounds like the job for you, you'll probably need a degree in graphic arts, advertising, or marketing. In addition to the training, knowledge, experience, and connections that come with attending an accredited program, you'll have the opportunity to begin building your professional portfolio. And you might even get the opportunity for some real world experience through co-op or internship opportunities. You might be able to get an employer to take a chance on you if you have a really excellent portfolio and the work

experience to convince them that not only can you get the job done, but you can get it done quickly.

Regardless of which way you get into the field, once you're there you need to do everything you can to stay on top of the changes and trends in the field of logo design. What colors are in, and which are out? What types of logos are companies leaning toward using? What can you do to make your logo designs stand out among all the others?

With talent and a lot of hard work, maybe someday one of your logos will be on the side of delivery trucks worldwide, on the front cover of the menu of a nationwide restaurant, or identifying a popular TV channel!

Pitfalls

You may have customers who are hard to please, or who don't like any of your designs. It's hard to work for clients like that, and it can be hard to take that kind of criticism about your work. Also, because it is easy to set up a logo design business, there is a great deal of competition from freelancers.

Perks

It's relatively simple and inexpensive for someone to open a logo design business. If you're already doing graphic design work, you probably own a great deal of the equipment that you'll need to get started. Also, it's nice to see your work in action on products and advertising.

Get a Jump on the Job

Take any graphic design classes offered at your school, and look into the possibility of taking summer classes at a local community college. Offer to create logos for your brother's band, the ice cream shop

Paul Browning, logo designer

L ogo design can be a tough field to break into because you need experience. "I got lucky," says designer Paul Browning. "I had a friend who worked for a print shop. They hired me to do T-shirt designs. They were patient with me while I learned the computer programs [needed to do the job]."

Eventually, he moved into designing illustrations and logos. "On-the-job training is a must, because school does not prepare you," notes Browning, who studied at Utah Valley State College and Brigham Young University. But he adds that you need to take classes to learn the computer software programs that are used in the design industry. Some things, however—such as dealing with people and developing good communication and phone skills—come with on-the-job experience.

A typical workday for Browning is eight hours spent designing logos at LogoWorks, a logo design service based in Lindon, Utah. He enjoys the creativity, the competition, learning about companies, and finding unique sources of inspiration. Browning also spends another hour or two each day freelancing. Most logo designers do some sort of graphic design work, but Browning points out that it's important to find a job that doesn't mind if you do work on the side. Most employers won't mind that you freelance, as long as your on-the-side work doesn't directly conflict with your day-to-day job.

Artistic students interested in graphic design should build a strong portfolio. "Do free work at the beginning if you have to, to get experience," Browning says. "You can't do this part-time and make any money, or even be that skilled. You need to immerse yourself in it."

your cousin owns, the school's chess club. Not only will you get some experience designing different types of logos, but you can also begin to build a portfolio. Be sure to collect letters of recommendation from the people for whom you do the logos.

MAKEUP ARTIST

OVERVIEW

Makeup artists work in a variety of settings, and with a variety of people. Some makeup artists work in television or theater, preparing actors for performances. Others work at the cosmetic counters of department stores and specialty shops, demonstrating how makeup should be applied. Some work with fashion models on photo shoots and runway shows, while others work for individual clients, such as brides. Cosmetic companies also sometimes hire makeup artists.

Whether you're working behind a cosmetic counter or behind stage at a top fashion designer's runway show, the job of a fashion designer is to color and beautify the client. You'll sometimes be asked to create a particular look, such as dramatically darkened eyes and lips. In other instances, you'll be expected to simply enhance the client's natural appearance.

Makeup artists who work in theater, film, or television face many challenges, such as lighting, making characters appear a particular age, or special makeup effects. Movie and theater makeup can be especially difficult because you may be expected to change the entire appearance of an actor by using rubber or plastic prostheses, wigs, or beards. Special training normally is required for this type of work. You also must be prepared to research styles and fashions of particular time periods in order to recreate a certain look.

Many freelance makeup artists, especially those just getting started, work a second job to make ends meet. Some work as sales representatives for cosmetics

companies, which can be beneficial because you remain within a related industry. Applying makeup for wedding parties is a growing trend.

Pitfalls

Working as a makeup artist can be pretty stressful, especially if you're working in a high-energy environment such as a theater production or a runway fashion show. Miscommunication between the

AT A GLANCE

Salary Range

The average national salary for a makeup artist is $32,550 a year, or $15.65 per hour.

Experience/Education

There are no formal educational requirements to be a makeup artist, but many have earned bachelor's or master's degrees in theater, art, film history, or another related area. Some makeup artists are licensed cosmetologists, which requires a degree from a technical school or two-year college. Experience working in theater is beneficial.

Personal Attributes

Should be creative, with artistic ability. Must be able to work closely with other people, in conditions that are sometimes pressured. A neat, clean appearance is desirable.

Requirements

You'll need a portfolio illustrating your work in order to get a job.

Outlook

Job growth of between 10 and 20 percent through 2012 is predicted, but this is a small field and many compete for available jobs. However, there is a rising demand overseas for American films, and the growth of movie rentals and the cable TV industry could mean increased demand for makeup artists.

Heather Fox, makeup artist

Heather Fox has worked with a long list of photographers, fashion designers, celebrities, musicians, models, and directors during the course of her career as a makeup artist. She also specializes in doing makeup for bridal parties, and has worked for magazines and live broadcast shows. With a background in cosmetic retail and modeling, makeup has been a part of Fox's life for a long time. Learning, however, is a constant project for her.

"I read books and magazines to keep up with trends and new techniques," she says. "I go to beauty school periodically to study a particular area of makeup. The more experience you get, the more you'll learn. It doesn't stop."

At the beginning of her career, Fox did makeup for wedding parties while working full time at another job. After getting some experience and discovering she was very good at makeup, she started networking with photographers in her area, joining forces to get more wedding jobs. She still enjoys doing wedding makeup, but has expanded her business to include many other areas.

Fox advises someone considering a career as a makeup artist to learn how to network. Meeting people such as photographers, models, and producers can jump-start your career and lead to still other contacts. A good portfolio is crucial, she explains, as are hours and hours of practice on yourself, friends, and family. You should expect to do a lot of makeup for free while building your portfolio. While Fox greatly enjoys her work as a makeup artist, she warns that it's not an easy profession.

"I would advise that being a media makeup artist for print, television, film, and video is not a glamorous job," she said. "It takes blood, sweat, tears, time, and money to get where you want to be as a successful artist for the big clients."

And, she warned, the competition is tough.

"Competition is pretty fierce because of the saturation of makeup artists out there," she said. "There are only a few successful artists in the field making six figures. But, if you're willing to work hard and pay your dues, and you really want to succeed, you may just do all right."

artist and the client or producer can result in a look that's different from what is expected and desired. And because competition for jobs is keen, you may need to begin working in jobs that aren't highly desirable or well paid.

Perks

If you like glamour and excitement, makeup artist might be just the job for you. High-profile makeup artists work with famous models, actors, and actresses, meet famous directors and producers, and are exposed to a world that many people never get a chance to glimpse.

Get a Jump on the Job

Any experience you get will help you to get into a school or enter the job market directly. Volunteer to help with makeup for school and community theater productions, and photograph all your work. If there's a community television studio in your area, volunteer to work there, applying makeup. And don't forget to take before and after photos of your clients. Once you're comfortable enough, volunteer to do makeup for your friends on special occasions, such as a prom or wedding. Save all the photographs you take—they'll be the start of your portfolio.

MURALIST

OVERVIEW

Imagine creating a mural that will last for 2,000 years or more! With the products and techniques muralists use today to create some of their paintings, it's possible their art will last for two millennia or more. What an awesome thought: Your work—a piece of you—will live on long after you have died, touching and inspiring many generations to come.

But first, the mural has to be created. The process starts when you meet the clients to find out exactly what they want. After the meeting, you will do some research. Depending on what the client is looking for (and your experience) you might research specific styles, periods, techniques, or even anatomy. Back in your studio, you'll do a scale rendering in color of the piece, and then you spend more time with the client, refining your sketch. Once the client signs off on the thumbnail sketch, you'll get a deposit, and the real work begins.

You'll probably spend one day getting the worksite ready. That includes getting the scaffolding, paint, and other equipment that you'll use in crating the mural. You'll also spend time protecting the flooring, furniture, and other objects in the room.

The next day you'll start sketching on the wall. Some muralists do this by hand, while others use a projector. For many beginning muralists, this is one of the hardest steps, because you have to work *big*, which is somewhat counterintuitive for an artist. If it's a small project, and you're confident in what you're doing, you might just start painting.

Once the painting begins, you'll probably work for a few hours, take a break for lunch, and work for a few more hours. Painting a mural is physically hard work, because you'll be up and down scaffolding countless times in a day. Taking a break helps you with your perspective.

Each mural will probably take you a week or two to paint, and you never want to break up one job with another job.

Gregg Bugala, muralist

Muralist Gregg Bugala has always been creative. At four years old, Bugala drew a picture of his baby brother that actually looked like his baby brother, complete with proper perspective—pretty impressive for a preschooler. Luckily, his parents recognized his talent and nurtured it. In fact, Bugala and his mom took art classes together when he was a child.

"I always wanted to make a living as an artist," Bugala says. He was willing to do whatever it took to make that dream a reality. Bugala worked in a bike shop to put himself through college. "[After college] I tried to be a freelance illustrator. When that didn't pan out, I made a living as a house painter, and then started doing faux finishing. I sold my art at fairs; I built houses; anything to get by."

Today Bugala does about 20 murals a year. But when he was just starting out, Bugala says, "I would work for next to nothing to get my name out there and build my portfolio. And I never turned down a job." And while Bugala has charged as much as $22,500 for a single painting, he did pay his dues as a struggling artist, and admits that things were really tough (financially) after the adoption of his first son.

For Bugala, one of the biggest perks is that "I can make a living doing what I love, and knowing that it comes from the heart." (To see some of Bugala's murals as well as his other work, visit his Web site at http://www.gregg-art.com.)

He puts a lot of himself into every painting, often adding little personal touches, such as a bug hiding in the crack of a faux finish stone wall, or the sun reflecting off a church steeple. He often pencils an inspiration or otherwise appropriate scripture verse onto the wall before beginning a mural. Those little touches are among the things that make his work special and unique. To be a successful muralist, Bugala says, you need something that sets you and your work apart.

"The more diverse you are, the greater the likelihood of getting jobs," he says. "Don't think you have it all figured out. There is a big world of art out there. Learn all you can about everything. Don't settle into one style, and you'll develop a style all your own."

It's much better to finish one job before moving on to something new.

At times, finding that next job can be difficult. Muralists never know where or what the next job will be. There may be slow times when they have to pound the pavement to drum up work, spending time sending out mailers and advertisements. It's often a good idea to drop a note to former clients asking for referrals. It's all part of marketing your work and yourself. Muralists sometimes take their portfolio to interior designers who might know of customers looking for custom work.

With this type of work, you're always looking for ways to expand your customer base. At times, you might have to paint things other than murals, such as faux finishing or decorative painting.

A college degree in art isn't necessary to be a successful muralist, but the more art classes you can take, the better. Art history is important because it will help give you background if clients ask for painting in different styles. A familiarity with art history also gives you a reference and starting point for the project. Classes in composition, drawing, and color theory are particularly helpful. Taking art classes beyond high school will also help you establish a relationship with other artists. You'll be able to build a community of your peers, which can be helpful when you need someone to brainstorm ideas.

As with most other creative pursuits, you need to be willing to pay your dues. When you're just starting out, be willing to work cheaply to get jobs so that you can build your portfolio. If you really want to work as a muralist, you'll need to be willing to work hard and do whatever it takes to be a success.

Pitfalls

It can be hard not knowing where your next job (or paycheck) is coming from. You'll have to deal with difficult clients, and sometimes you'll have a client you simply can't please, no matter what you do. Other times your clients really don't care about your art; they're using you as a status symbol.

Perks

As a muralist, you'll have the opportunity to make a living doing what you love, and at the same time, create works of art that touch people. To some extent, muralists can set their own hours, depending on the client. Every day is different.

Get a Jump on the Job

Look for classes and workshops in mural painting and other painting techniques. Check for after school and summer opportunities at local community colleges or art centers. Investigate books on different painters, painting, styles, and techniques. Learn to work on a large scale. If possible, spend a summer working for a mural painter.

PACKAGE DESIGNER

OVERVIEW

The bright orange package of Reese's Peanut Butter Cups, the dark blue cylindrical box that shouts Morton Salt, the little plastic egg containing Play-Doh—each of these packages is so memorable, most people can recognize them from size, shape, or color alone.

That recognizability means that somewhere, some package designers have done their work very well. One of the goals of a successful package designer is to make that package recognizable.

There are two sides to packaging design, both of which require a creative streak, but one of which is much more technical than the other. One type of package designer creates the actual package in which an object is sold. You might design a certain type of box, bag, bottle, or other package to accommodate a particular item. The other type of package designer creates a decorative look for that box, bag, or bottle. Sometimes, the same person might do both jobs.

While these jobs go hand in hand, they are very different, with different sets of requirements and expectations. When designing actual packaging, you've got to consider factors such as tamperproofing, making the package strong enough to protect the contents, cushioning factors, and other aspects. Skills involved with this side of packaging design include science, math, sociology, business, and psychology.

AT A GLANCE

Salary Range

$25,000 to $100,000 annually, depending on experience, location of work, and other factors.

Education/Experience

A bachelor's of science degree or bachelor's degree in art or design is usually necessary.

Personal Attributes

You must be adept at problem solving and able to think creatively. You should also be able to work effectively with others and to communicate ideas easily.

Requirements

Experience in design, good math skills, and the ability to be able to envision a three-dimensional object made from two-dimensional materials.

Outlook

Careers in packaging design are expected to increase at an average rate of between 10 and 20 percent through 2012.

If you want to make the packaging look attractive so that people want to buy it, your skills must be more art-based. There are other aspects of this side of package design, however. For instance, you'll need to know how to comply with government-mandated labeling requirement for consumer goods, which include restrictions and specifications as to how packages are labeled, sizes of packages, and so forth.

Basically, a package designer in the artistic sense tries to make an attractive, eye-catching package to grab the attention of prospective customers. Cereal boxes, for instance, must be immediately recognizable to kids, who in turn will pester their parents to buy a particular brand. Think about the bright

Forrest Watson, package designer

Forrest Watson is a corrugated designer who works in the technical side of package design, but he refers to his profession as a craft. Watson, who has a bachelor's of science degree in packaging, works in the corrugated field—in other words, he designs corrugated packages such as boxes and heavy wraps.

Watson designs packaging to meet the specific requests of his customers. If he's designing a box that will hold a computer, for instance, he must figure out how to keep the computer from being damaged during shipping, how to separate different components of the computer within the box, and so forth. Designing a box that will hold a metal file cabinet is much different, as you can imagine, from designing a box in which fine crystal will be shipped.

Watson, of Temecula, California, enjoys the actual design work involved with his job, but he isn't as anxious to deal with customers and salespeople.

"My job is never boring because I'm doing different things all the time," he says. "And I'm always seeing new products. "

Watson advised someone interested in packaging design to go to a school that offers an applicable degree—but don't expect to land a top job right after graduation, he warns.

"A degree in packaging will give you good base knowledge, but most of the training is learned on the job," he explains. "This is a craft that takes time—through years of experience—to learn. You don't come out of college having the experience to be a proficient designer. So, you have to be willing to work hard and to start out at low pay."

orange box that General Mills, Inc. uses to package its Wheaties cereal. The color of the box is certainly no accident. An artistic package designer decides the size and type of print to be placed on a package, package color, and the best means of letting customers know what the package contains. If you've ever picked up a package and had to read every bit of print on it to determine its contents, you know how important it is for packaging to be clearly labeled and easy to read.

Packaging designers who create packages usually work for manufacturing companies, such as a corrugated box manufacturer. Packaging designers whose job is to make the package attractive may work for a package design firm or on a freelance basis for housewares companies.

Pitfalls

Neither the technical nor design component of packaging design has traditionally been a fast-growing field, and advancement within the field may be slow.

Perks

Happily, the industry is expected to perk up, due to additional work inspired by government regulations.

Get a Jump on the Job

Keep up with packaging trends by being aware of the style and design of packaging in housewares, grocery, electronic, and other stores. Retail work will give you a close-up look at how packaging works, as well as what is considered attractive and saleable.

PHOTO RETOUCHER

OVERVIEW

The expression "what you see is what you get" is catchy, but it doesn't hold true when it comes to photographs. Although photo retouching has been used almost as long as there have been photographs to retouch, sophisticated, readily-available computer equipment has made it easier to retouch photos, and more difficult for the average eye to detect the changes. The job of a photo retoucher is to change the appearance of photos using tools such as special paints, airbrushes, and specialized computer software.

If photo retouching sounds like fun to you, you could find work with an ad agency, design house, entertainment company, magazine, or photographer, or you could be hired by somebody looking for someone to *touch up* a portrait or wedding or family photo. You'll be trying to make sure the photo produces the image that was intended. As a result, it's very important that you understand where the photo will be used, who will see it, and what its intended message will be. But that's not all—there also are technical aspects to consider: Colors and images appear differently on different media. For instance, the same photo looks different on a glossy magazine page than it does when printed on a cardboard box or a billboard. Factors such as ink densities and linescreen must be considered.

You'll need to understand specialized software that allows you to remove or add items to a photo, blur images, add

motion, change colors, clean up photo backgrounds, and make flat objects appear three-dimensional. In some ways, you get to play fairy godparent, removing reflections, whitening teeth, and making eyes sparkle. You also can make composite photos, which combine parts of more than one photo to make a new photo. Of course, all of these changes require special techniques and expertise. For this reason, some employers require a degree in art, photography, or computer science, while others will look primarily at experience and qualifications.

David Mackay Ballard, photo retoucher

Trained as a graphic artist, David Mackay Ballard got into photo retouching during the 1980s through a job with a graphics agency. The agency produced the covers of a series of trade magazines, and Ballard was given the responsibility of making them look perfect.

"Obviously, you want to get rid of any flaws in a photo that's going to be used on the cover of a magazine," Ballard said. "It was part of my job to do that, but it was mainly a trial-by-fire kind of thing."

Ballard, of Berlin, Massachusetts, now has his own freelance business. While photo retouching is part of his job description, he also does animation and illustration projects. Most of his photo retouching jobs are generated through advertising agencies, with which he's developed work relationships. Ballard highly recommends that anyone interested in photo retouching gets some sort of art degree, and not limit him or herself strictly to photo retouching.

"A degree certainly helps," he said. "I'm sure there are people who are doing graphic art and photo retouching without a degree, but you usually can tell. If you can get training and experience in more than one art area, you'll be more attractive to employers and have a better chance of getting the work you want."

Once you're established in the business of photo retouching, you can think about starting your own business or working on a freelance basis. While photo retouchers are found throughout the country, jobs are more concentrated in cities, where there tend to be more advertising agencies, photographers, design houses, and so forth. If you're working on a freelance basis, you may find more jobs if you consider a variety of job sources instead of concentrating on just one area. Some photo retouchers also work as photographers.

Pitfalls

Jobs for photo retouchers can be pretty competitive, and you might have to be willing to relocate if there aren't many jobs in your area. Until you've been in the field for a while and have established contacts, you could find it difficult to get enough work. You're also likely to find yourself working within some very tight deadlines. If you're working for an ad agency, your work will be viewed and critiqued by art directors, so a top-notch product is necessary.

Perks

If you love art, photography, and technology, what could be more fun that being a photo retoucher, which combines elements of all those areas? Chances are that you'll work with people who share your interests. If you work on a freelance basis you'll be able to have some flexibility in your schedule, although you'll need to satisfy the demands of your clients.

Get a Jump on the Job

Learn all you can about the tools and software used in photo refinishing. Learn how to work with photo software programs such as Adobe Photoshop, which allows you to experiment with retouching photos. Try to put together a basic portfolio of your work, which you can display electronically on a site such as AF WORK (http://www.allfreelancework.com).

POTTER

OVERVIEW

If you're interested in being a potter, you're joining a long line of artists! Folks have been producing pottery since ancient times. In fact, the oldest known grouping of pottery known is thought to have been made in the years between 10,000 and 400 B.C. Although pottery designs are continually changing, basic pottery techniques have not changed much. The success of a piece of pottery depends largely on having the correct composition of clay, having adequate skill to mold the clay or shape it while it's wet and on the potter's wheel, and knowing how to fire the piece at the proper temperatures.

While shaping and molding a piece of pottery is the nuts and bolts of a potter's work, decorating the piece is the icing on the cake. A potter must have a good knowledge of glazes, both those used for utilitarian purposes and those used strictly for decorative purposes. There are many types of glazes, all with special properties and uses. Many potters also paint decorative designs on their works, combining drawing and painting skills with their pottery expertise.

Many, many items are crafted by potters. While we may think primarily of pitchers, bowls, and plates as being potters' wares, potters also create ceramic tiles, candlestick holders, lamp bases, vases, and other utilitarian and decorative items.

While making pottery is an extremely satisfying process for many people, it is neither fast nor easy. If the work is done entirely by hand, the potter creates a piece by either throwing the clay on the

AT A GLANCE

Salary Range

The median salary for a salaried potter—that is, someone hired by a company to make pottery—is $35,260, with the lowest 10 percent of salaried potters earning less than $16,900 and the top 10 percent earning more than $73,560. The earnings of freelance potters vary tremendously, depending on experience, location, and demand for the work. More than half of all potters work on a freelance basis.

Education/Experience

Most professional artists, including potters, hold a degree in fine arts or a related area, or at least have extensive training in pottery. Studio experience is also necessary.

Personal Attributes

Creative, artistically skilled, and patient. Must be willing to work long hours to succeed. Need upper body strength to throw wheel.

Requirements

Should have a knowledge of the history of pottery, and be interested in different historical styles of pottery. Need a strong desire to succeed as a potter and be willing to practice extensively.

Outlook

Employment for artists of all types—including potters—is expected to grow by between 10 and 20 percent through 2012. That is considered average growth.

potters wheel in order to create the desired shape, molding it by hand, or molding it with a form. The piece is then left to dry, a process that can take from three to 10 days, depending on the size of the object. The work then undergoes an initial firing, called a *bisque firing*, after which it is glazed and fired again. Some pieces are glazed twice, requiring an extra firing.

Wesley Muckey, potter

Wesley Muckey grew up in a family where art and music abounded. Someone nearly always had a painting or other artistic work in progress, and the house was usually filled with sound from an instrument or voice. "It's a family thing," says Muckey. "We were a very artistic and musical family."

Muckey's first love was oil painting, which he learned from a family friend when he was about 14 years old. A few years later as a high school student, however, he discovered a new love—pottery.

"I knew almost right away it was what I wanted to do," says Muckey. "It was exciting. I loved working in 3-D instead of with a flat painting. And I loved that there are no limits. You can make anything with clay."

The owner of a pottery shop, who also happened to be a teacher at Muckey's high school, observed his student's obvious talent as a potter and offered him a job. Muckey was 16 years old when he started making pottery in his teacher's shop, and he ended up staying there for 15 years.

He attended college during that time, majoring in art, but didn't earn a degree. Instead, he said, he took what he needed to know from his classes and kept on making pottery, becoming more and more skilled over time.

"I was lucky to get the training that I needed, and then to have a chance to work at it all the time," he says. "Pottery is a trial and error kind of thing. The best thing to do is get a wheel and just work constantly on it."

Muckey and his partner, Greg Zieber, have a special interest in recreating historical pottery. They copy museum pieces, or extensively research a particular type of pottery and recreate it. Some of Muckey's favorite pieces to make are face jugs, which were originally made by slaves in the South.

"They say that these were originally made to be whiskey jugs, and they'd put really scary, awful faces on them to keep the children away from the whiskey," says Muckey. "That's one theory about these jugs, and it's our favorite one. We're really into the historical background of the pieces that we make."

Muckey now works from a studio in a barn behind his rural home in Angelica, Pennsylvania, inspired by the woods behind him and the creek that runs through his property. About half of the pieces he makes are commissioned by customers, while the other pieces are crafted as time permits, then stored to be exhibited and sold at the three shows they hold throughout a year.

Recently, Muckey was happily working on a set of 81 tiles, each depicting a scene from the Noah's Ark story. When finished, the tiles will be mounted and framed for a client.

"It's a lot of hours," says Muckey. "And sometimes I'm up in the middle night firing the kilns so they'll be ready to go. But, I don't look at what I do as work, because I just love it. I've been lucky to get to the point where I am, but I just hope to keep working and getting better and better at what I do."

If you're looking for instant gratification, making pottery may not be for you. It can take from three to four weeks to complete one piece of pottery. If you love working with clay, however, and seeing your artistry expressed in a three-dimensional form, you're not likely to mind the wait.

Potters often work for themselves; some work in co-op settings with other artists and potters, while others work on their own in their own shops. Some are commissioned by clients to create pieces, while others make works that are sold at craft shows or in consignment or craft shops. Some potters get contracts to produce works for department stores or specialty shops. Those who aren't self-employed may be hired to work for busy potters who need extra help.

Regardless of how you end up working and selling your work, you'll need to be willing to work hard and long to establish yourself and have your work become known and recognized. Some potters establish a distinctive style that sets them apart from others and appeals to a certain segment of buyers, while others attempt to create more mainstream pieces that may have a broader appeal.

Pitfalls

Being an artist is a tough way to make a living, at least at first, and pottery is no exception. Being able to buy the equipment you need to get started may be difficult.

Perks

Creating is fun, and being able to make a living from selling what you create can be extremely rewarding and satisfying.

Get a Jump on the Job

If you can, buy a potter's wheel and some clay, and start practicing. If you can't get you own wheel, try to find a workshop or pottery-making class where you can have access to one. If there's a pottery shop nearby, ask if you can watch the potters work, or volunteer to do small jobs for them so you can spend time there.

RESUME WRITER

OVERVIEW

You have a degree, and maybe you even have several years of experience under your belt. But when it comes time to look for that new job, the most important tool you need to develop is a terrific resume. Resume writing can be tough—many people find it hard to know what to say about themselves. That's where a professional resume writer comes in.

A good professional resume writer works with the client to identify his or her key selling points, and then crafts a focused and compelling resume that really works. Professional resume writing is much more than typing a document—a good resume writer is a true strategist whose job is to craft a high-impact sales message on the client's behalf.

Everybody has unique skills, abilities, and talents, but only a truly creative approach to resume writing can highlight what is uniquely special about a person. Today, resume writers not only craft written, traditional resumes, but also interactive online portfolios, videos, and other interesting electronic products.

Resume writers must have a keen eye for a good graphic design, since research suggests a person's resume has less than 20 seconds to make the right impression. To get the best bang for your buck, it's important that a resume be eye-catching and easy to read.

To be effective, a resume must be much more than a straightforward accounting of a client's career. It must be a unique marketing document that highlights the person's key skills and minimizes anything that might be seen as a liability, such as

lacking a key area of experience or having long gaps between jobs. A resume writer must understand the current job market, the needs of recruiters and hiring managers, and the best ways to present a client's background to match these needs.

Typically, professional resume writers will sit down with a client (or conduct an interview over the phone) to try to figure out exactly what the focus of the resume will be. The resume writer also must learn what kind of the job the client is looking for.

Many people don't know that there are professional certifications for resume writers. These certifications are only earned after rigorous testing, and those who hold the qualification must adhere to a stringent ethical code. A resume writer

Sandra Lamb, resume writer

Sandra Lamb always liked research and investigation, and turned those abilities into a lucrative ability to write professional resumes for job seekers.

Lamb started out as a technical writer, writing instrumentation manuals to help lab technicians assemble equipment. It was very good experience in building up a thought process, and in teaching her the value of action words. What she loves about resume writing is that she can help "distill somebody's real skills."

Starting out, Lamb specialized in writing resumes for people whose experience was "outside the box" or who were re-entering the job market—especially newly divorced women. "I helped them look at their experience and evaluated their skills so they could produce an effective resume," she explains. "There was a disconnect in being able to apply life experience and skills they had in the workforce." In fact, this is work she particularly loved. "About 90 percent of these women didn't value their own life skills. They didn't value that they managed to get two kids through college, that they managed an annual budget for the family, making all those executive decisions."

She began working with friends and acquaintances, and then as word spread began to volunteer her services to newly divorced women entering the workforce. "Once you start, it's truly a word-of-mouth business," she explains. Although she advertised in the newspaper in the beginning, she quickly found that advertising just wasn't necessary as more people heard of her skills. She specialized in working with people with unusual skills, such as artists, who needed something more creative to showcase their abilities. "A functional resume won't tell you what a graphic designer is capable of," she explains. She also began helping job seekers create disks and video resumes, and in posting creative resumes on Web sites.

Lamb, who is also the author of *How to Write It: A Complete Guide to Everything You'll Ever Write*, advises people to "think of the job hunting process as a job in itself. It takes real effort," she says. When working with a person's resume, Lamb focuses on figuring out what specific job they want and what problem the job is trying to solve. "I ask, 'What solutions can this person bring to help solve this problem?' Think of a resume not as a set document, but as a toolbox."

can be certified as either a CPRW (certified professional resume writer) or a NCRW (nationally certified professional resume writer.)

Pitfalls

Resume writers must work with all kinds of people and learn to be enthusiastic on paper about someone they may not like personally.

Perks

There is a continuing huge market for new employees and hence, a big market for experts who can help job seekers craft impressive resumes. Opportunities abound for talented freelancers who like the independence of working for themselves.

Get a Jump on the Job

The best way to hone your resume writing skills is to write a lot of resumes. Try taking some books out of the library and studying up on various resume styles, and then start crafting some of your own. Play around with graphics on your computer, and see what you can come up with.

SAND SCULPTOR

OVERVIEW

If you've ever visited a beach, chances are you've spent some time playing in the wet sand at the water's edge. Some folks build castles, others use a stick to sign their names, and most leave deep footprints along the water's edge. Even if you've never seen the ocean, odds are you've spent some time as a child creating sculptures in a sandbox.

While building a castle out of sand is part of a relaxing afternoon in the sun for most folks, for a talented few it's not just fun—it's also serious business. Professional sand sculptors spend weeks turning tons of sand (between 10 and 5,000 tons) into breathtaking sculptures.

Believe it or not, people actually earn their living building sand castles! These performance artists can carve just about anything you can imagine out of a block of sand to provide entertainment at fairs, festivals, shopping centers, and other special events. And lest you think sculpting sand is just child's play—it's not uncommon for a professional sculptor to earn $8,000 to $10,000 for an average sculpture consisting of 50 tons of sand and a week of carving time.

These amazing works of art start with sand and water, and while each artist or company may have a formula (in terms of a sand-to-water ratio), that's all that the pros use—no additives, binders, or chemicals are added to hold the sand together. Not even a squeeze of Elmer's.

The mixture of sand and water is poured into a form (or mold) of just about

AT A GLANCE

Salary Range
A journeyman sculptor with three to fours years of experience can expect to make about $300 a day. Most sculptors work an average of 180 days a year.

Education
None required, but a solid knowledge of math and architecture are important.

Personal Attributes
Good communication and interviewing skills. Sculptors should be patient, methodical, detail-oriented, and able to work while under close observation.

Requirements
None.

Outlook
Sand sculpting as a profession is still relatively new. There are about 150 to 200 professional world-class sculptors; about 40 live in North America. Experts predict continued growth in this field.

any shape and size, and then tamped down. Then the sand-filled forms are layered or stacked on top of each other to create the basic form from which the sculpture will be built. Now the magic begins!

Starting at the top of the sculpture, the sculptor removes the wooden form around the sand and carves the top layer. Moving downward, each form is then removed and carved. Sculptors use a variety of tools, including things you might find in your own kitchen (such as pastry knives and even drinking straws) and your tool box (small shovels, trowels, and soft-bristled paint brushes).

But it's not all fun in the sun for sand sculptor! They work in all sorts of weather,

Ted Siebert, sand sculptor

Lots of people wish they could turn their hobby into their profession and actually make a living at it. Unfortunately, for most people it really isn't an option. Ted Siebert is definitely an exception to the rule. "If you work hard," he says, "you can succeed at anything!"

Siebert started entering amateur sand castle competitions in the Seattle area as a hobby when he was 29 years old. Teaming up with some others who shared similar interests, the group went on to win many sand sculpting titles, including the World, National, United States, and Canadian Championships.

Today, Siebert works full time as a professional sand sculptor. In addition to numerous championships, Siebert and artists from his company (The Sand Sculpture Company) hold a total of six world records in the *Guinness Book of World Records,* including the world's tallest sand sculpture (24' .02") and the world's longest sand sculpture (6.53 miles). (You can check out some of Siebert's award-winning sculptures along with pictures of some of his other creations at http://www.sandsculpting.com.)

While Siebert admits sand sculpting is a lot of fun, he notes it's not all effortless. Now 46, Siebert says he's seen much younger sculptors quit because of the hard work. "We work long days, 9 to 10 hours a day," he says. "More if we have a deadline to meet. It's hard work, and very physically intensive labor."

When a sculpture is complete, Siebert says he feels a huge sense of accomplishment. "It's amazing to step back and think: 'I built this with my own two hands.'" The fact that his sculpture won't last more than a year doesn't really bother him. "It's so rewarding to complete a job," he explains, "and I know there will always be another job. But, the bigger the job, the harder it is to walk away."

Even for those who may not want to make a career out of being a sand sculptor, Siebert notes that working with a professional sculptor for a summer can be a great job, and learning how to work with your hands can be great experience no matter what career you might choose.

"You don't have to be a classically trained artist to do this," Sieber says. "Anybody can do it! Be enthusiastic and put effort into it. You can accomplish anything if you try."

good and bad. Sculptors work in searing heat, wind, and rain. In adverse conditions, a completed sculpture might be treated with a water repellant to help it last longer. Some sculptors have even braved blizzard conditions to travel to the location of an indoor event! These indoor sculptures can last for a year or longer.

Each September, the best of the best vie for the title of world champion. Sculptors descend upon Harrison Hot Springs, British Columbia, where they spend up to 100 hours (depending on the category) creating breathtaking, awe-inspiring works of art. The event is only open to master sculptors (individuals who have worked with a professional sand sculpture company for at least three years, or meet other very specific requirements). In addition to the prestigious title of world champion, the top sculptors walk away with several thousand dollars in prize money.

If you decide to become a professional sand sculptor, you probably won't need a college degree to get a job, but what you will need is experience. There are many ways you can get that experience. One of the simplest, most basic things you can do is to practice at home. Build a large sandbox in your backyard (large enough to hold several 30-gallon trash cans worth of sand) and start sculpting. Experiment with different tools and techniques to find ways to get a certain look.

When it comes time to look for a job, you might apply to one of the several sand sculpting companies, or you could try striking out on your own.

Pitfalls

Much of your work will be outdoors, in all types of weather—so you'll be dirty all the time. Sometimes you may have to work on a sculpture that just isn't your cup of tea. At times, the work gets monotonous.

Perks

As a performance artist, you'll get to enjoy the reactions from your audience—and you'll have the opportunity to travel all over the world. People will enjoy your work, and you will receive lots of compliments. And unlike many forms of art, sand sculpture is fairly lucrative.

Get a Jump on the Job

Learn to draw. Any art background is helpful, so take whatever classes are available to you so that you can learn the fundamentals. Then, practice, practice, practice. There are several good books on the subject, plus lots of how-to advice on the Internet. Many sand sculptors have Web sites with photo galleries with pictures that may inspire you—and that might give you some ideas for your own creations. You also can take lessons; a number of professional sculptors teach the art of their craft. Once you've learned a variety of skills and techniques, you might be able to apprentice with a master sculptor.

As your skills improve, volunteer to do small-scale sculptures for local events like school fairs, fund-raisers, civic events, and festivals. If you have the opportunity, enter local, amateur events to start gaining recognition. Look for opportunities to work for or intern with a sculptor during your summer vacations from school.

STAINED GLASS ARTIST

OVERVIEW

If you've ever stood in a cathedral in Europe and gazed in awe at the magnificent stained glass windows—such as the famous Rose Window in the Notre Dame Cathedral in Paris—you've got a sense of the incredible possibilities in stained glass art.

Of course, these days many stained glass artists work in much smaller scale—creating window panes, hanging art, lamps, and so on. But the process is often very similar. Most stained glass artists work as freelance craftspersons in their own studios, choosing their own designs and exhibiting and selling their work in craft shows or in art galleries.

As a stained glass artist, your first job is to pick a pattern and the glass. Thousands of stained glass designs are available in books as full-size patterns, complete and ready to use—or you can come up with your own designs. Once you've chosen a design, you number the pattern, cut it apart, and trace the pattern onto the glass. After scoring the glass, you then break out the pieces and grind them to fit your design. Next comes foiling—you pull a length of foil tape from the roll and peel back two inches of the protective paper backing. Next, you press the sticky end of the foil onto the glass edge, leaving exactly the same amount of overhang on either side. All foiled joints must be completely soldered to create the metal web that will hold your project together.

There's some initial expense up front when you begin working in stained glass.

AT A GLANCE

Salary Range
$20,000 to $60,000+

Education/Experience
A background in art or design is helpful; many small colleges or community colleges teach classes in stained glass.

Personal Attributes
Patience, artistic eye, attention to detail.

Requirements
None.

Outlook
Fair.

You need a variety of tools such as scorers, pliers to break glass, a grinder to grind glass to different shapes, foil, and solder. If you use a kiln, that alone can be more than $1,000.

Pitfalls

Initial outlay for equipment can be expensive, and the work can be tedious. There are also some safety issues in stained glass art, especially for those who work with lead. Stained glass artists should never eat food or smoke when working. You should always wash your hands, and don't put your hands in your mouth.

Perks

As in most art forms, stained glass can provide a fulfilling way to live a creative life. Stained glass artists are usually self-employed, and therefore enjoy the freedom to create their art and explore different areas while earning a living doing what they love to do.

Liz Cresap, stained glass artist

Many artists start out in one creative area, and eventually branch out into their life's work. Such was the case with Liz Cresap, a stained glass artist who thought she was going to be an interior designer. She earned a degree in interior design from the University of Maryland, and with her flair for design, she got a job in visual merchandising display at Hecht's Department Store. For several years, she also worked as floral designer.

But it was a class in stained glass that got her interested in a new art form. Soon she was selling pieces at a florist's shop. "That's when I thought I could make money doing this."

Today, Cresap, of Crownsville, Maryland, is the owner of a stained glass business, The Glass Rose—named such "because glass is fragile, like a rose," she explains. At the moment, she's working on a commissioned piece—a sailboat for a 50th wedding anniversary gift. Now specializing in fusing glass with a kiln, Cresap has been working in stained glass for the past 20 years, and specializes in pendants, bowls, and candleholders.

Once busy attending craft shows, she's now affiliated with a small art gallery, and gets commissions and referrals. Today she's working on fusing wine bottles by placing them in a kiln, which flattens them out. She got into fusing because she was starting to see the same stained glass things at craft shows, repeating themselves.

"I like to design my own patterns, but I kept seeing the same patterns over and over," she explains. In the past, when she was designing stained glass for a craft show, she'd have to make many of the same pieces. Eventually, this grew tiresome, she says. "I can't stand mass production," she explains. "I just want to be creative and do unusual things."

Creating and working with stained glass can be tedious, Cresap says. "You have to stick with it, and don't be afraid to break the glass. Just jump in and do it!"

Still, it's an art form that Cresap finds always enjoyable. "I love it when people receive their pieces," she says. "They're always happy, and that makes it really fun and rewarding. That's what I like the best about the job."

Get a Jump on the Job

To see if stained glass is for you, check into local classes at a community college near you or at retail stores that sell supplies. You also can find stained glass classes announced at the SGAA Stained Glass School at http://www.stainedglass.org.

TEXTILE DESIGNER

OVERVIEW

Textile designers are specialized artists for whom technical knowledge is also important in some cases. While many people think of textile designers as those who create the pictures and patterns that decorate fabric, there actually are different types of textile designers. Those who create the flowers or other prints that adorn fabric are called print designers. They're basically fine artists who specialize in fabric.

Another type of textile designer is a weave designer, who figures out weaving patterns and properties. A weave designer needs to have a better understanding of how fabric is made and the technical aspects of fabric than a print designer, so different types of education may apply. A print designer may need a degree in fine arts, while a weave designer might benefit from a degree that incorporates the technical aspects of textiles, such as a science degree.

You probably think of clothing when we think of textiles, but textile designers also design items for the home, such as furniture, table linens, bedding and towels, or even design flooring or wallpaper. The same design company might handle projects ranging from punk-style T-shirts to delicate floral sheets.

A portfolio highlighting your work is a must in getting a job as a textile designer. If you attend a textile school, you'll probably have a considerable portfolio by the time you graduate. It's important to know and keep up with color trends and customer

wants concerning graphics and textiles, for, as you know, fashion is never static.

Many textile designers work on a freelance basis, but jobs also are available in textile mills, department stores that carry their own labels, stores such as Target and Pottery Barn, apparel companies such as Eddie Bauer or L.L. Bean, textile companies such as Burke Mills, Inc. or Avondale Mills, flooring companies such as Armstrong World Industries, and houseware producers such as Pfaltzgraff.

There are colleges across the country that offer degrees in textile design. Because

Nancy Eiseman, freelance textile designer

Nancy Eiseman started out in college as a math major, but changed schools after a year and ended up with a degree in fine arts. Eventually, she earned a master's degree with a concentration on the scientific aspects of textile design. This learning allowed her to combine her artistic talents with the technical knowledge and skills necessary to be a textile designer who specializes in woven textiles.

"It's a very technical field," says this Swarthmore, Pennsylvania, designer. "I don't just design the print on the fabric, I design the fabric, as well."

While artists called print designers create the prints and patterns that adorn fabric, Eiseman starts at the beginning and designs the weave of the fabric, which is a more technical job.

"I'll figure out the best weave for a particular item, choose the border size for an item such as a towel or tablecloth, select the fabric . . . I normally am hired to design an entire piece," Eiseman says.

She always loved fabrics and sewing, but didn't realize when she was in high school that textile design could be a career. "I wish someone would have told me that," she says. "I always was interested in this as a career, but I didn't know it was an option."

Eiseman advises anyone interested in becoming a textile designer to find a good design school and earn a degree.

"There are a lot of things you really need to know how to do," Eiseman says. "Trying to be a textile designer without earning a degree would be like trying to be an engineer without the proper training."

However, it's possible to get into textile design without a degree in textile design.

"If you want to be a print designer, you may be able to get started with a related degree, such as painting," she says. "Textile design is kind of a broad field."

Eiseman has been a freelance textile designer for six years, and has no trouble finding work. Her clients include well-known companies such as Pillowtex Corp./Fieldcrest, and DuPont. Although she usually sketches, draws, and paints to work out her ideas for a fabric item, she uses a textile computer-aided design (CAD) program to complete a job. She likes the CAD program, she said, because it allows her to easily created and view color patterns, design flawless repeats, and edit her artwork quickly. Because the system is digital, it allows her to quickly get design files to her clients for their review. "Working with the CAD system gives my clients many advantages," Eiseman says.

It's also important for a textile designer to work closely with clients, and to be sure that you understand a client's needs and expectations before beginning a job. Your designs, Eiseman says, must match your clients' visions.

competition for textile designer jobs can be tough, it's important to choose a good school where you can get a degree that's geared specifically to the type of textile designer you plan to become.

Pitfalls

There's a lot of competition for jobs in textile design. If you choose to be a free-lance designer, you might have to hold an additional job in the beginning in order to make enough money. Some textile designers have trouble balancing the artistic elements of the job with the technical and scientific elements. It's important to know what different types of textile designers do when charting your college and career path.

Perks

Working in the textile industry gives you a front row seat when it comes to new trends and fashions. In some aspects of textile design, you get to come up with an idea for a design, and see the design through to the finished product.

Get a Jump on the Job

If you don't already know how to sew, find a class or someone to teach you. Become as familiar with possible with different types of fabrics, perhaps through a job in a fabric store. Research colleges and pinpoint those that offer good textile design programs.

VIDEO GAME DESIGNER

OVERVIEW

If you've ever spent an action packed afternoon squealing around the racetrack as the mushroom-headed driver in *Mario-Kart*, you know the appeal that a great video game can have. Video game designers develop the concept, layout, and design of a video or computer game, writing the framework, laying out the theme, mission, and rules. But, unlike other storytellers, a video game designer provides twists and choices that allow players to determine how the plot will unfold.

Designers usually work in teams. As a lead game designer, you'd be responsible for the overall concept of the game, and would write a detailed plan describing everything that occurs. The plan, called a design document, includes maps of every game setting, descriptions of everything a player will see or do during the game, and flow charts illustrating how events progress. This is why good writing skills are crucial for a video designer. It's not enough to be able to visualize a game—you must be able to communicate that visualization.

The lead designer then works with artists, musicians, sound designers, and programmers to produce the game. The number of members in a development team can range from a dozen or so to more than 100, depending on the complexity of the game and the amount of money the publishers is willing to invest in it. In some cases, millions of dollars are invested in the development of a video game.

AT A GLANCE

Salary Range

Between $40,000 and $80,000, with an average salary of $61,403, according to a survey of video game designers.

Education/Experience

Although a college degree is not always required, most game designers earn one (usually in English, art, or computer science). Most video game designers get into other areas of the gaming industry first, and move into game design once they're established. More available jobs in the video industry include game artist, programmer, game tester, and producer. Some companies hire junior designers, but even those jobs usually go to people already working in the gaming industry.

Personal Attributes

Creativity is essential to a video game designer, but you must also be able to communicate your creative ideas effectively, both in writing and verbally. You must have strong technical skills, knowledge of gaming, and a feel for what makes people want to play video games. And because designer jobs are among the toughest to find within the gaming industry, perseverance and patience are pluses.

Requirements

None.

Outlook

Good. Americans spent $10.3 billion on video games, game players and accessories in 2002, and the spending is expected to continue increasing. Video development companies, which employ video game designers, are growing swiftly as demand for new games continues. Best places to break in are Los Angeles, Silicon Valley, San Diego, Austin, Tokyo, Seoul, or England.

Although there's a lot of artistry in designing video games, a designer must

Tom Sloper, video game designer

Tom Sloper has designed games for companies such as Sega Enterprises, Inc., Datascan, Inc., Atari Corporation, and Activision, Inc. Based in Los Angeles, where he's president of Sloperama Productions (http://www.sloperama.com), he's currently a consultant, author, and speaker.

Throughout his career as a game designer and producer, Sloper developed electronic games and toys that have generated more than $176 million in sales. If you're interested in being a video game designer, Sloper suggests you get a four-year college degree in a topic you find interesting—he recommends courses in physics, psychology, drama, literature, art, mythology, and (of course) computers.

He notes there's nothing wrong with starting out in the quality assurance (Q.A.) segment of the video game industry, working as a game tester. While some aspiring game designers look down on that job, Sloper says it's a great way to break into the business. "A job as a game tester gives the aspiring designer a grunt's-eye view of the game industry and also shows company management the work ethic of the aspiring designer," he says. "I am personally acquainted with game vice presidents who started in Q.A."

have technical skills, as well. To be a successful video game designer, you need to understand how games work, which means having a grasp of computer programming and software design. Management skills also are important, because the designer usually is in charge of the development team and must incorporate many ideas into a single product.

Pitfalls

Competition for video design jobs is high, and many game publishers won't hire a designer who doesn't have at least a game or two to his or her credit. As a beginning video game designer, you may be assigned to a low profile, low-budget game.

Perks

Once you're in, you'll enjoy a good salary and be able to work in a casual environment with other creative people. If you love video games, what could be a better job than designing them for others?

Get a Jump on the Job

Your first step toward becoming a video game designer is to get your foot in the door of the electronic gaming industry. Some community colleges and technical institutes offer courses on the gaming industry, and some video game firms offer nonpaying internships.

VIOLIN MAKER

OVERVIEW

Violin making is a highly skilled craft, involving many steps and procedures. Unless you're lucky enough to have been raised at the knee of a violin maker, you'll need to go to a school where you can learn how it's done. Some violin makers are self-taught, but most have specialized training. In the United States, there are schools that specialize in violin making in Chicago, Boston, and Salt Lake City, along with specialized schools in England, Germany, Italy, and Switzerland. There are many areas of knowledge necessary in violin making, including types and qualities of woods, varnishes, tone, and historical versions of instruments.

Many violin makers also make other stringed instruments, such as violas and cellos, along with stringed instrument repair. There is a process to violin making, and a sequence of steps that must be followed requiring great accuracy and attention to detail. If you combine violin making with instrument repair, you'll need to find a way to balance the two jobs, perhaps dedicating several days a week to repairs and the rest of your work time to creating.

If you're trying to break into violin making, you might consider working in a shop or factory that mass-produces instruments. Although most violin makers prefer to make an entire instrument, working in a shop can provide experience and teach you how the parts of the violin fit together, the qualities of different woods, and so forth.

While an established violin maker generally gets business through word of mouth, you'll need to be able to promote

yourself when you're just getting started. If you repair instruments, you might be able to get started in business by contacting music instructors in the schools in your area. Students and parents often ask music teachers for advice if they have an instrument that needs repairs.

Apprenticing for an established violin maker is a great way to learn the craft and

David T. Van Zandt, violin maker

David T. Van Zandt was busy studying voice at a music school when he decided to change direction and become a violin maker. So, he enrolled at the Violin Making School of America in Salt Lake City, Utah, and learned to make and repair violins, violas, and cellos.

"I was a musician, but I never would have made a living out of it," he says. "And I was good with my hands. Violin making seemed to fit my personality."

Twenty years later, Van Zandt has crafted more than 90 instruments, which (depending on the type) sell for between $12,000 and $24,000. For most of those years, he also did repair work. It was only after his business prospered and demand grew for his violins that he was able to give up the repair work.

Although Van Zandt has been successful as a violin maker, he warns that the work is difficult. "It's a job, there's no way around it," he explains. "I have to work 9 to 5 just like everybody else does. It's difficult to make a living making violins."

Van Zandt advises anyone interested in becoming a violin maker to get sound technical training at a specialized school. "The people who make their livings at this [violin making] have very good technical skills," he says. "And they have good people skills because they need to be able to sell themselves and their work. They have business skills so they can be successful and take care of themselves. It's a three-legged stool and you've got to have those three skills."

"I'm too curious about violins and varnish and woods and sound and music to do anything else," he says. "That's why I do this."

establish contacts, but opportunities to apprentice are very limited. Most violin makers are self-employed, which appeals to people who don't want to be forced to keep to "normal" business hours. And, many who make and repair musical instruments also sell equipment and supplies.

Pitfalls

Handmade violins are luxury items, and the demand for them is relatively small. If violin making is your only means of income, you may have trouble earning enough money. Moreover, people who hire professional violin makers are likely to expect high standards, which can cause significant stress. You'll be expected to meet deadlines and maintain a high level of quality in your work, while also having to run the business and promote yourself while keeping up with billing, paperwork, and taxes.

Perks

If you love crafting objects with your hands, you may find great personal and professional satisfaction in making violins. Often, you'll be able to set your own schedule. Creating something beautiful is tremendously rewarding for many people, and greatly appreciated by customers who recognize the skill required to do so.

Get a Jump on the Job

The first thing you can do is learn to understand the mechanics of a violin and how the pieces are put together. If possible, get a job in a music shop that sells and repairs instruments, and get to know the person who does the repairs. Express your interest and ask if you can observe his or her work. Also, look into schools that specialize in violin making.

WAX MUSEUM STUDIO ARTIST

OVERVIEW

A clutch of famous Hollywood actors are congregating at a cocktail party in small groups, when suddenly a tourist comes up from behind and hugs Brad Pitt. Not a raised eyebrow among the bunch—and why? Because this particular cocktail party takes place at Madame Tussaud's Wax Museum in New York City, and every one of the guests is an oh-so-elegantly coiffed and dressed wax figure.

The job of the studio artist—whether as a wax sculptor, hairdresser, costumer, or painter—is to build a series of frozen moments, and to make those moments as believable as possible. Many things go into making these wax figures believable: the way the clothes are placed, the coloring on the hands, the drape of a shirt or jacket, how to show tiredness, how a haircut is feathered.

The studio artist must figure out how to get a reaction from people, making the figures as alive as possible from head to toe. To do this, each figure must be moved each day, the clothing altered a bit, the hair tousled. From time to time the hair must be washed and styled, since the artists use real human hair, which gets dirty over time depending on the weather and the number of visitors tousling the hairdos. If the hair—which must be individually inserted, hair by hair—isn't applied properly, it won't lay right and won't look right.

What makes the figures so challenging is that all the bodies are different—no body is quite the same, no skin is quite the same

color. The sculptors build an armature of aluminum piping to hold the clay with which they model the figures; the heads are then worked on the body at first to get the correct positioning, then they are taken off for finishing.

A plaster of Paris mold of the head is made, then a molten beeswax mix is poured into it, cooled, and set. It's basically the same process and the same kind of wax that's been used since the founding of the wax museum about 200 years ago. However, these days, the bodies are molded in resin and fiberglass; originally, they were made of leather stuffed with straw.

Pitfalls

Artists say it's hard to see their work deteriorate; when a figure is first created it's clean, fresh, and alive, but over time it begins to break down. You're also not likely to get rich working on wax figures,

Nicholas Carbonaro, wax museum studio artist

Nicholas Carbonaro had no idea when he was taking art classes at Ithaca College that one day he'd be producing elegant hairdos for mannequins made of wax. "But the more you know, the better off you are. I think it's important to have a liberal arts or fine arts background. To be an artist, you need to understand history, social sciences, math—you need to know a lot about the world around you to create art that depicts that world."

After Nick moved back home to New York City to look for work, he happened to walk by Madame Tussaud's one day. "New York is such a visual city," he notes, "that if you're a young art graduate and you walk around, you'll find ways to apply your skills." He started as a host, until he went to his boss and asked for a chance to work on the figures. "I know I can pick this up," he said, "so give me a chance." Although not trained specifically as a hairdresser, he was good at multitasking. "You can't go to school and major in wax museums," he notes. "But how to make a figure look fresh, alive, human—it's all in your eye. I've learned so much by seeing things, which enabled me to come back and reflect the quality of a person's body, the way he holds his hand. Those things make you believe a figure is real."

Carbonaro's job is to observe the figures to give the visitor the best experience possible. "How do you make Alexander Graham Bell look pensive as he's sitting in a chair?" Carbonaro explains. "If the hair looks too neat, people will touch it, they won't believe it. "

And the more real the figures look, the more the people will interact with them. "It's like a great big psychological puzzle," Carbonaro says. "They react as if the figures are alive. They'll get excited to see their favorite star, they'll give him a hug. That's my job."

"All of us [studio artists] sit on the subway and stare at people," Carbonaro laughs, "so that we can make the figures lifelike. When people bump into one, they'll say 'excuse me!' It's not just a bunch of figures in a room, getting dusty."

"I love what I do, and I'm constantly being challenged," says Carbonaro.

and it can be challenging for an artist to have to work with and please the corporate side of the business.

Perks

The work is unusual and always different, creative, and fun—and keeps artists on their toes. Combining many different skills into one position, it's also a good way for young artists to broaden their skills base as they build their resume and portfolio.

Get a Jump on the Job

Any kind of artistic experience can be a springboard for this job, but particularly helpful are experiences in theater, makeup, set design, costuming, fabrics, hairdressing, sculpture, painting, colors, and design.

WEDDING GOWN DESIGNER

OVERVIEW

While the names of high-end designers like Vera Wang, Amsale Aberra, Ulla Maija, and Reem Acra might come to mind when you think of wedding gown designers, there are thousands of lesser-knowns who design beautiful gowns to be worn by radiant brides. A wedding gown designer is a specialized fashion designer who can work for an apparel company, specialty stores, or high-fashion department stores, or directly with clients to design one-of-a-kind wedding dresses. Some work in elegant bridal shops, while others operate out of their homes or have tiny shops.

Because a wedding gown designer gives birth to dresses that follow or even predict market demands and trends, a successful designer must be tuned in to fashion trends and cultural influences and be able to anticipate the direction in which styles will go. The trick to fashion design, including wedding gowns, is to create styles that customers want—before they even know they want them.

Designing wedding gowns for an apparel company that markets them to wholesalers and retailers is a much different prospect than designing gowns for individual clients. When you work for an apparel company, you'll be expected to design dresses that appeal to many. If you design gowns for individual clients, the only person you need to please is your client.

Being able to work easily with others is especially important to a wedding

gown designer. If you're part of a work team, you'll need to be able to effectively communicate your design ideas with pattern makers and sewers. If you work directly with clients, good people skills will be particularly important, as a wedding gown is a personal and emotionally charged item. And a woman who hires someone to

Rachel Kurland, wedding gown designer

Rachel Kurland has been making dresses for brides, bridesmaids, mothers of brides, and others for 20 years, and now owns Foxglove Custom Bridal Gowns in South Strafford, Vermont. With a background in costume design, Kurland began designing and sewing custom wedding gowns when her children were small and she wanted to be at home with them.

"I wanted to stay home with my kids, so I put a screen door on my studio and went to work," Kurland says. "That way, they could see what I was doing, but they couldn't get in to get peanut butter on the white dresses."

A friend asked her to share the cost of an ad in a wedding magazine, which got Kurland her first jobs. From there, word of her work spread, and she has sewed hundreds of dresses since.

"I create dresses not only for brides, but for mothers of brides and bridesmaids, too," she says. "And, I restore mothers' wedding gowns for daughters to wear. So I've made hundreds of dresses, but not all of them have been wedding dresses."

While Kurland very much enjoys designing and sewing wedding gowns, she says the work isn't for everyone. Pressure runs high when there's a wedding coming up, she says, and some brides tend to suffer from overly high expectations.

"A lot of people get burned out making wedding gowns because the people you're working for are under so much pressure," Kurland says. "And some people expect that when they put on a custom-made dress, they're going to be a fairy tale bride. That isn't always realistic."

Kurland makes all her gowns twice—once from muslin or another inexpensive material, and the second time from the satin or other fabric the bride has chosen. The first dress, a mock-up, allows the bride to experience the fit and how the dress falls, and lets Kurland make adjustments, as necessary.

"Sometimes we find that the design just doesn't work exactly the way we thought it would," Kurland says. "Having the muslin version allows us to change the design so that the wedding gown is exactly what the bride wants."

The price of Kurland's gowns varies greatly, depending on the fabric used and other materials needed, and the complexity of the project, but she tries to work within the budgets of her clients.

Kurland's education was in costume design, and she has a master's degree in fine arts, but she recommends that anyone interested in wedding dress design look for a fashion school to attend. A course in fashion design, she said, teaches all the skills necessary either for working for someone else or going into business for yourself.

"They teach you how to render and market and price," Kurland says. "Because my background was costume design, I never learned those skills and I had to try to pick them up along the way. I can build anything, and I can sew something that will make someone look good and also feel comfortable. But, to this day, I don't have a clue about marketing."

Still, Kurland has no plans to stop designing and sewing wedding gowns.

"I love working with the brides, and I love sewing and working with fabric," she says. "My mother taught me to sew when I was about three years old. Time has always passed quickly for me when I was sewing, and it still does."

create a one-of-a-kind wedding gown is likely to have strong ideas about what she wants and how it should be done.

Until you've established yourself as a wedding gown designer and clients are knocking at your door begging for your creations, you'll need to market yourself and your designs. It's essential to have a good portfolio that highlights your best work. If you start your own business, you'll need to think about advertising in one form or another.

Pitfalls

Creating wedding dresses sounds dreamy, but it can involve significant periods of stress as you're pushed to meet deadlines and satisfy the demands of nervous brides-to-be. Some designers feel stifled when they must change what they feel is the perfect gown in order to satisfy the expectations of a client. Others have difficulty staying organized when it comes to ordering supplies, meeting with clients, and meeting tight deadline demands. In addition, breaking into the specialized field of wedding dress design can be difficult.

Perks

Who wouldn't love to create gorgeous dresses that draw *oohs* and *aahs* from wedding guests and are photographed extensively, and carefully preserved for wear by future generations? Wedding gown designers get a tremendous amount of satisfaction from pleasing their clients. If you work for individual clients, you'll have a high degree of flexibility and working options, which many people find attractive.

Get a Jump on the Job

Apprenticeships are great for aspiring wedding gown designers. If you can't find a wedding gown designer in your area, apprenticing for another type of fashion designer also will provide excellent experience. Work to get a good portfolio together, and learn all you can about the fashion industry and wedding industry. A job in a wedding salon would be a great way to learn about fabric, fit, and design.

WINDOW DRESSER

OVERVIEW

While most people think of a window dresser as someone who designs and decorates the show windows of large department stores, window dressing occurs in a variety of settings and circumstances. As a result, if you're considering window dressing as a career, you should be open-minded about the opportunities that are out there. Hotels sometimes employ window dressers, as do some museums, wine and spirits distributors, bookshops, and film and television studios. Window dressers also are employed to design exhibits at trade shows and exhibitions. Still, department stores hire more window dressers than any other industry.

A window dresser (also known as a visual merchandiser or merchandise displayer) plans and sets up commercial displays. In addition to designing and setting up displays in windows, a window dresser often is also expected to address the interior design of a store, which involves arranging merchandise to feature certain items and to best attract customers. If you would get a job as a window dresser for a chain department store, it's likely that you'd be based in the main store or company headquarters and travel from store to store to coordinate exhibits and work with staff.

Design jobs attract creative, artistic types, but you'll need to be in good physical condition if you're planning to be a window dresser. You'll spend a lot of time on your feet, and be expected to

climb ladders to work on sets and lighting and hang materials. The job also involves lifting and bending to arrange floor designs. You also need to be willing to have flexible work hours and to work overtime during

Kim Slocum, window dresser

Kim Slocum was never formally trained as a window dresser, but she's been working as one for 25 years. A combination of luck and artistic talent got her into the business and has kept her there, learning the trade from other window dressers as she went along. She got her first job when, recently graduated from high school, she packed up some of her artwork and paid a visit to a window dresser at a department store in Ann Arbor, Michigan.

"I always had an interest in art, and I had done a lot of sketching and painting," she says. "I heard that Jacobson's Department Store in Ann Arbor was looking for a window dresser, so I took my paintings and drawings and stuff down there, and the little man who was there hired me. Then I learned from him about window dressing. I was just really lucky to have met people who were willing to train me."

Slocum worked for various department stores during the years since her first job in 1979, including Neiman Marcus. About eight years ago, she decided to strike out on her own.

"It's been a learning experience," she says. "Freelancing is a lot different than being employed by someone else. My problem is the business end of it. I hate dealing with the business side, but it's really important to pay attention to that and make sure everything is in order. If you don't, you get disorganized and let things slip, and then people can take advantage of you."

Among Slocum's clients in Pinckney, Michigan, are jewelry stores, hair salons, an import store, individually owned boutiques, and several Louis Vuitton stores. She also decorates homes and businesses for holidays and parties.

"I decorate people's Christmas trees and mantles during the holidays," Slocum says. "And I work with a company that decorates for theme parties. I also have a wine store and I decorate stands for trade shows. And, I own a lot of props that I rent when I can. When your work is freelance and can be unpredictable, you have to have some options to fall back on."

Slocum enjoys seasonal decorating, using props from her large and varied collection to create different themes throughout the year. She also depends on her collection to create themed windows, such as a jungle or underwater look.

While Slocum never had formal training as a window dresser, she says those aspiring to work in the field probably should consider training at a design school in order to increase their chances of getting a job. As with most professions, window dressing has changed in the past 25 years, and employers may not be willing to hire someone with no specialized schooling or training, she says.

holidays—the times during which the most attention is given to a store's windows.

Of course, a window dresser must be up-to-the-minute with what's happening in the fashion world, and be knowledgeable of cultural trends and current events. You also will need to understand the corporate culture of the company for which you want to work, and know the image the company works to portray.

Other skills necessary to window dressing are an understanding of lighting and special effects, knowledge of computer-aided design (CAD) and 3-D design and the ability to use software to plan and implement design. You'll also need to be able to communicate and work well with others, and be organized enough to work well in advance of an upcoming season or event and to coordinate the handling of merchandising materials.

Pitfalls

Because your work is on display for everyone to see (and potentially to criticize), there is a fair amount of stress associated with being a window dresser. You'll run into some tight deadlines that will require you to work long (and often unusual) hours. Remember that many storeowners prefer that their windows be dressed during hours that the store is closed. Beginning window dressers often start at a fairly low salary. And, since a high percentage of window dressing jobs are in cities, the cost of living there could be higher than what you can comfortably afford. You'll be in for some stiff competition when applying for a job, especially if you're looking to work for a high-end department store.

Perks

Despite the long hours, stress, and hard work, many people desire to be window dressers. Why? Because it's fun. And you get to express your creativity and artistic talent for all the world to see—or at least all passersby to see. Window dressing attracts talented, creative people, who generally enjoy working with other talented, creative people. So, you're likely to be in good company. There's room for advancement in the field of window dressing, and, because it's a topic that interests many people, some window dressers have gone on to write memoirs or books about the art of window dressing. Once you're established as a window dresser, there are opportunities to work on a freelance basis or serve as a consultant.

Get a Jump on the Job

Visit your career planning and placement office to learn about the possibility of internships in the field of window dressing. Most colleges encourage internships for qualified students and will assist you in finding one. If you're still in high school, you might contact a department store directly to see if any learning opportunities exist.

WOOD-CARVER

OVERVIEW

Wood carving has been traced back at least as far as the year 1000, and was prominent in temple and palace architecture. While woodworking generally involves machines, wood carving is almost always done by hand, even if some power tools are used. Wood carving is an art that also demands technical skills.

Wood carving begins long before your chisel meets wood. It begins with a vision—an idea of what your finished work will be. In fact, beginning to carve wood without a completed design already in your mind is a recipe for failure. Designing your carving can, and often does, take longer than the actual carving process. If you're making a carving for someone else, it's extremely important to fully understand the customer's expectations before you begin the work. It's good to make sketches of the work you're visualizing to be sure that you and the customer have the same vision of the completed work.

Experienced wood-carvers tell of the need to feel the piece of wood you'll be carving while visualizing the finished work. This allows you to fix your image of the work into the wood, and will guide you as you work.

Wood-carvers use a variety of tools, including knives, chisels, and gouges. Different types of tools are used for different tasks. A straight gouge, for instance, might be used for removing large areas of background wood and making curved surfaces, while a bench knife is used for shaving wood and rounding edges. A general knowledge of the tools is

necessary to begin woodcarving, but you'll develop your own preferences as you gain experience.

As with all types of artists, most wood-carvers are self-employed, and many have other jobs to supplement their carving business. If you're thinking about wood carving, be realistic about your potential earnings and judge whether you'll need to have a second job. If you're planning on being on your own as a wood-carver, you'll

Joe Leonard, wood-carver

Joe Leonard is a highly regarded wood-carver from Garrettsville, Ohio, perhaps best known for his carousel horses. His hand-carved horses are so popular, in fact, that Leonard was hired to make 17 of them for the carousel in the EuroDisney theme park outside of Paris. He worked for a year and a half on that project, hiring four people to help.

His carousel horses, however, aren't his only triumphs. Leonard refers to a carved version of Pegasus, the mythological flying horse, as his signature piece. The winged horse is nine feet long and eight and a half feet tall, with wings that extend more than six feet upward. Commissioned by an Ohio client as a Christmas gift for her husband, the work is carved from basswood and painted with enamels; the horse's armor is decorated with gold and silver leaf.

"Even now, if I take someone to that house to show them that work, I can hardly believe that I was able to make something like that," Leonard says.

Leonard did not set out to be a wood-carver, but instead chose a job in the advertising field. It was after he met someone who had a damaged carousel horse that his career began to turn down another path. Leonard agreed to try to repair the broken legs of the wooden horse. He did so, and then decided to try to carve a horse. One thing led to another, and today Leonard is not only a popular and sought-after wood-carver, he also leads wood-carving seminars and writes for publications geared toward wood-carvers.

Leonard is a freelance wood-carver who works mostly on commission—clients hire him to carve a particular piece. That means that he needs to have a very clear understanding of the exact piece the client wants, and be able to communicate effectively throughout the carving process. He takes ongoing photographs so clients can see their pieces in progress.

"That's how most of my work is done," Leonard says. "On occasion I get ahead and make a few pieces that I can sell through a dealer or something. But mostly I work on commission."

While Leonard loves his work and is grateful for the recognition and acclaim it has brought to him, he makes no pretense that it's easy or glamorous. Still, he says, the thought that people are willing to pay him handsomely for his creations is inspiring.

"This is very much a job," Leonard says. "Often it's from 7 in the morning until 10 at night, and I don't get all that much carving done because of interruptions and other matters I need to tend to. But, the rewarding thing is when someone commissions me to do a piece and is willing to pay me $18,000 or $20,000 or $25,000 for something I make. That's very gratifying."

Leonard advises anyone considering wood carving as a career to take classes and seminars if you can find them. They're sometimes offered through local wood-carving shops. Seek out local carver's clubs, and join the National Wood Carvers Association. If there's a wood-carving supply shop in your area, check it out. Not only will you find tools you'll need, but you'll meet others who are interested in woodworking, as well. There are some woodworking books available, and a few instructional videos that might be useful.

Then, Leonard advises, be patient. It can take years to become established as a wood-carver, and years more to build up a clientele. Treat your customers well and try to be patient with their demands.

Leonard offers one final bit of advice to aspiring wood-carvers: "Everybody must have a leather thumb protector," he says. "If you don't wear one, keep the Band-aids handy. You'll need them."

need to have some business skills to be able to deal with customers and effectively run your business. Many artists find it difficult to keep up with the business end of their operation. A business course or even a good book on starting and running a business is recommended. Also, some chambers of commerce or other community groups offer free consultations with retired business owners for people looking to get started in a business. The Small Business Administration (http://www.sba.gov) is another useful resource.

Pitfalls

Until you're established and your reputation has spread, you're likely to find it difficult to make a living as a wood-carver. It's true that some wood-carvers enjoy a very high standard of living, but many have to find other work to supplement. You'll also need a studio, or at least a well-equipped workshop, and the necessary tools with which to operate, which could be initially costly.

Perks

If you like working with your hands and love wood, then you're likely to love a job as a wood-carver. As you know, personal satisfaction is extremely important when choosing a career. And you're sure to meet interesting people, both in the clients you'll have and the fellow wood-carvers you'll meet if you join an artists' guild or group.

Get a Jump on the Job

If you know a wood-carver, ask if you can watch him or her work. Visit a nearby lumberyard and ask for scraps of woods with which to experiment. Read books about wood carving and learn all you can about different types of wood.

YARN HAND-DYER

OVERVIEW

In this busy, always-on-the-go society, traditional needlecrafts such as knitting and crochet are becoming more popular than ever. But it's not just little old ladies in rocking chairs picking up their needles and hooks—it's Hollywood movie stars, high school students, corporate executives, and just about everyone in between.

After a hectic day grappling with the office printer, struggling to keep your computer from crashing, or arguing with the marketing department, people want to do something relaxing with their hands. Some folks prefer to nest, spending more time home with their families. Others want to create heartfelt gifts for their loved ones. For these special gifts, ordinary yarn just won't do. Quite often these knitters and crocheters want something special—something that expresses their personality. Many of them find exactly what they're looking for in skeins of beautifully hand-dyed or hand-painted yarns.

The hand-dyers or artists who create the amazing color combinations (called *colorways*) are often inspired by the world right outside the studio windows: the soft pastels of an early spring flower garden, the red-hot colors of a steamy summer sunset, or the steely grays found in the sky before a storm. Some dyers say that colors come to them in vivid detail in their dreams. Others look though magazines for colors, combinations, and shades. Still others admit to finding inspiration through a trip to the local shopping mall, energized by the people, the colors, the sights, the sounds, and the smells. No matter what the source of the inspiration, once an artist has an idea, it's off to the studio to turn that idea into reality!

Creating a skein of yarn that captures the hand-dyer's vision often takes many attempts with different colors and different combinations. For example, a first attempt might produce a purple that's too red. Hand-dyers make adjustments until they have exactly the right shade to match the inspiration. It's not just a matter of getting exactly the right colors—it's also arranging those

Cheryl Potter, yarn hand-dyer

Cheryl Potter grew up in Maine in the 1960s, during the era of tie-dye and crochet. "Everyone in my family was into crafts in a big way," Potter says. "I did lots of crafts at home as a child." Ironically, she took no art classes in high school, but while a student at Middlebury College in Vermont, she did custom knitting—making hand-knit garments to earn extra money. During that time, she was first introduced to hand-dyed yarns.

"I graduated without any idea what to do," she recalls. "I was good at everything, and there was no job description for what I liked to do." So, it was off to graduate school in Arizona, where she was introduced to the hand-dyed yarns used by the Navajo nation. Potter eventually earned a master's of fine arts in creative writing from the University of Arizona, and promptly took off for Nepal, where she hooked up with rug weavers and learned about dying with plants.

Throughout her knitting career, Potter grew frustrated that no one had the colors she wanted to use. Eventually, she began dying her own yarn. After dying her yarns for several years, she was "discovered" in 1997 by major knitting magazine *Interweave Knits*. Before the article, Potter had been selling her yarns out of a room in a large farmhouse where she ran a bed and breakfast; afterwards, she received so many cards and letters from people interested in her yarns that she quit her job and started doing retail shows.

"There was no niche for me, no job out there. I felt like I wasn't good enough at any one thing," she says. "This is what I was meant to do. This is what I am the best at." Potter's business, Cherry Tree Hill, has grown from 80 accounts in 1998 to more than 600 today. She still works 50 to 60 hours a week creating colorways, dyeing yarn, and handling the administrative side of the business. (You can see some of the unusual yarns Potter dyes, along with her gorgeous colorways, at http://www.cherryyarn.com.)

"Be open and willing to take a chance," she advises students considering a career creating hand-dyed yarns. "Ignore peer pressure. Trust your own judgments about what's going to work or not going to work. Do what you like, and believe in what you do."

colors in a pleasing order. The hand-dyer might find that putting a blue-purple color next to a dark green produces a muddy-looking patch where the colors blend. It's important to spend time arranging the colors so that the entire skein of yarn looks good, with appealing colors and blends.

Once the hand-dyer is happy with the colors and the combination, the formula or recipe must be recorded. Most hand-dyers keep detailed records not just of their successes, but of their trials and errors. Each time a new colorway is started, there's a reference to consult.

After a colorway is perfected, the hand-dyer will create multiple skeins of that colorway. (How long, and how many, depends in part on the size of the hand-dyer's business.) A hand-dyer who sells only out of the studio will obviously produce fewer than a company supplying 100 retail stores.

If creating luscious colors in yarns appeals to you, you can attend classes or workshops to learn how to use the chemical-based dyes and paints safely. This also will help you master different techniques to produce different results. Once you learn the basic techniques, it's a matter of trial and error to create your favorite colors and colorways.

Pitfalls

You need lots of money to get started as a hand-dyer. Depending on the size of your business and how quickly it grows, you may be forced to spend time dealing with administrative issues, which leaves less time for creating new colorways and dyeing yarn. As a business owner, you're at the mercy of the customers' wants, trends, and the seasons of the year.

Perks

Yarn hand-dyers get the opportunity to explore and experiment with different colors and fibers. Creating the raw material for someone's work of art, it's fun to see your yarns worked up into different projects, especially in patterns and magazine articles.

Get a Jump on the Job

If you're tempted to tint, you can start out creating your own hand-dyed wool yarns using unsweetened powdered drink mix. It is a quick, safe, nontoxic way to experiment with colors and combinations—right in your own kitchen. Directions can be found on the Internet by searching for "Kool-aid yarn dyeing."

When you're ready to try your hand using professional dyes on a variety of different fibers, there are many different workshops that will get you started with the basics. These workshops are usually held at knitting conventions or fiber festivals. You can usually find information on yarn dyeing classes in knitting magazines or on the Internet. Alternatively, look for an opportunity to spend a summer working for a hand-dyer. Learn as much as you can not only about the creative side, but about the business side too!

APPENDIX A. ASSOCIATIONS, ORGANIZATIONS, AND WEB SITES

ANIMATOR

The Animation Learner's Site
http://come.to/animate

A one-stop guide to learning how to animate, with tutorials on animation and drawing, as well as other resources like books and technical supplies to help you out. There are also a few articles written by real animators and other animation-related workers.

Animation Magazine
30941 West Agoura Road Suite 102
Westlake Village, CA 91361
(818) 991-2884
http://www.animationmagazine.net

A magazine focused on the business, technology, and art of animation.

Animation School Review
http://www.animationschoolreview.com/
animation-resources-links.html

List of animation schools in the United States, by state.

Animation World Network
6525 Sunset Boulevard, Garden Suite 10
Hollywood, CA 90028
(323) 606-4200
http://www.awn.com

The largest animation-related publishing group on the Internet, providing readers from over 145 countries with information on all aspects of animation, including animator profiles, independent film distribution, commercial studio activities, animation technologies, and in-depth coverage of current events in all fields of animation.

SIGGRAPH
http://www.siggraph.org

A diverse group of researchers, artists, developers, filmmakers, scientists, and other professionals that share an interest in computer graphics and interactive techniques. SIGGRAPH's parent organization is the Association for Computing Machinery (ACM), the world's first and largest computing society. ACM serves as an umbrella organization for information-technology professionals. SIGGRAPH sponsors not only the annual conference, but also focused symposia, chapters in cities throughout the world, awards, grants, educational resources, online resources, a public policy program, traveling art show, and the SIGGRAPH Video Review.

ARCHITECTURAL ILLUSTRATOR

Robert Becker, Inc.
Conceptual Design and Architectural
Illustration
53 Parklane Drive
Orinda, CA 94563-3236
(925) 254-4234
http://www.robertbecker.com

Robert Becker has been an architectural illustrator since 1986. His Web site in-

cludes views of his work, his biography, and his thoughts on collaborating with clients and a client list.

Lawrence Technological University
21000 West Ten Mile Road
Southfield, MI 48075-1058
(800) 225-5588
http://www.ltu.edu

Lawrence Technological University is one of the few U.S. colleges to offer a four-year program in architectural illustration. Students who graduate from the course receive a bachelor's of fine arts in imaging. The university is located in the Detroit metropolitan area.

ART CONSERVATOR

The American Institute for Conservation of Historic & Artistic Works
1717 K Street, NW, Suite 200
Washington, DC 20006
(202) 452-9545
info@aic-faic.org
http://aic.stanford.edu/contact.html

The national membership organization of conservation professionals dedicated to preserving the art and historic artifacts of our cultural heritage for future generations. The organization provides a forum for the exchange of ideas on conservation, and advances the practice and promotes the importance of the preservation of cultural property by coordinating the exchange of knowledge, research, and publications.

The Canadian Association of Professional Conservators (CAPC)
c/o Canadian Museums Association, Suite 400
280 Metcalfe Street
Ottawa, Ontario

Canada K2P 1R7
(613) 567-0099
http://www.capc-acrp.ca

The professional body that accredits conservation professionals in Canada. Founded in 1971, CAPC works to establish and encourage high standards of competence, integrity, and ethics in the field of conservation.

Canadian Conservation Institute (CCI)
1030 Innes Road
Ottawa, Ontario
Canada K1A OM5
(613) 998-3721
http://www.cci-icc.gc.ca

International organization dedicated to conservation that produce publications and organize professional meetings.

Heritage Preservation (HP)
1730 K Street, NW, Suite 566
Washington, DC 20006
(202) 624-1422
http://www.heritagepreservation.org

Group that provides a forum for discussion, understanding, and awareness of national conservation and preservation needs. HP offers bibliographies and other publications on a wide range of conservation and related topics.

Getty Conservation Institute (GCI)
1200 Getty Center Drive
Los Angeles, CA 90049-1684
(310) 440-7325
http://www.getty.edu/conservation/institute

The institute addresses conservation problems of cultural property through its programs in scientific research, training, documentation, and publications and its administration of the Conservation Information Network (CIN).

The International Institute for Conservation of Historic and Artistic Works (IIC)
6 Buckingham Street
London WC2N 6BA
England
(011)+44(0)2078395975
http://www.iiconservation.org

International organization dedicated to conservation that produces publications and organizes professional meetings.

ART DEALER

Art Dealers Association of America (ADAA)
575 Madison Avenue
New York, NY 10022
(212) 940-8590
http://www.artdealers.org

A nonprofit membership organization of the nation's leading galleries in the fine arts. Founded in 1962, the ADAA seeks to promote the highest standards of connoisseurship, scholarship, and ethical practice within the profession. The ADAA members deal primarily in paintings, sculpture, prints, drawings, and photographs from the Renaissance to the present day. Each ADAA member is an experienced and knowledgeable dealer in his or her field. The ADAA has 160 member galleries in more than 25 U.S. cities.

BALLOON SCULPTURE ARTIST

Ballooniversity
http://www.ballooniversity.com

Each summer, balloon professionals descend upon the town of town of Athens, Georgia, to attend Ballooniversity. Sponsored by Flowers, Inc. Balloons, Ballooniversity offers individuals the opportunity to learn from some of the top experts in the balloon industry.

Balloon Camp
http://www.ballooncamp.com

You can learn the ins and outs of working as a balloon professional at Balloon Camp in Las Vegas. Balloon Camp offers classes in balloon twisting, business and retailing, and balloon decorating. Participants can take part in evening twister jams—where twister artists share their skills in a non-classroom setting.

Balloon Hat
http://www.balloonhat.com

In 1996, balloon twister Addi Somekh and photographer Charlie Eckert set out, traveling around the world making balloons hats for people. Even if you aren't particularly interested in balloon twisting or balloon hats, the Web site is worth a visit to see picture of the places they went, the people they met, and the incredible balloon creations that they made.

Balloon HQ
http://www.balloonhq.com

Balloon HQ is a huge source of information about balloons and balloon art. You'll find professional resources like a guide to balloons and ballooning, photos, monthly columns, event coverage, an artist directory, and more. You can connect with other balloon professionals, both entertainers and decorators, through the forums and discussion lists. There are links to facts and fun where you can find some sculpture basics and an extensive list of balloon-related books and videos, learn the history of balloons and how they are made, and more. The Balloon Council Web page is housed at the Balloon HQ site, http://www.balloonhq.com/Balloon Council.

Balloon Images
5000 East 29th Street North
Wichita, KS 6722-2111
(800) 803-5380 (press 2)
http://www.qualatex.com/pages/
resource_catalog/bimagescatalog.php

Balloon Images *magazine is published four times a year by Pioneer Balloon Company (maker of Qualatex balloons). Each full-color issue is packed with classic balloon décor ideas, marketing and business information, tips, techniques, ideas, and more. Back issues are available.*

Balloon Magic
http://www.balloonmagic.com

Marvin Hardy is one of the premiere balloon twisters in the world. His Web site is a terrific source of information for anyone interested in balloon art. Be sure to check out the balloon art gallery at http://www.balloonmagic.com/balloonartgallery.html.

International Balloon Arts Convention (IBAC)
http://www.ibaconline.com

The International Balloon Arts Convention (IBAC) is a professional convention for people working in the balloon industry. Attendees take classes, create pieces for competition, and take part in other special events. Participants also have the opportunity to gain some hands-on experience working with some of the best balloon artists in the world to create event décor. Check out the photo album at the IBAC Web site for pictures of past winners in the various categories.

Pioneer Balloon Company
5000 East 29th Street North
Wichita, KS 67220-2111
(800) 803-3315
http://www.qualatex.com

Each year, Pioneer Balloon Company manufactures almost one billion latex balloons sold under the name Qualatex. Pioneer is one of the largest manufacturers of latex balloons. They are leaders in the balloon industry, and are the developers of the Certified Balloon Artist (CBA) program (http://www.qualatex.com/pages/cba_info.php). The Qualatex Web site has information and links of information for anyone considering a career as a balloon artist or balloon entertainer. You can find color charts to help you plan your designs, instruction sheets, information about shows and events, balloon industry news, lots and lots of photos, and much more.

BOARD GAME DESIGNER

Board Game Designers Forum
http://www.bgdf.com

Online form for professional board game designers featuring Web resources, chat rooms, game journals, and discussion forums.

Board Game Invention Web site
http://spotlightongames.com/list/design.html

This Web site has it all: information on designing games, lists of companies buying games, forums, bulletin boards, and much, much more.

BOOKBINDER

Information about apprenticeships and other training opportunities may be obtained from local printing industry associations, local bookbinding shops, local offices of the Graphic Communications International Union, or local offices of the state employment service.

Bindery Industries Association, International
100 Daingerfield Road
Alexandria, VA 22314
For general information on bindery occupations.

Graphic Communications International Union (GCIU)
1900 L Street, NW
Washington, DC 20036
(202) 462-1400
http://www.gciu.org

BUMPER STICKER WRITER

Humor Writers
http://www.humorwriters.org

University of Dayton's Erma Bombeck's writers' workshop, this Web site includes lots of information on contests, newsletters, workshops, and links.

CALLIGRAPHER

Calligraphy by Nan DeLuca
Greenwich Village
New York, NY 10012
(212) 477-3732
http://www.scribenyc.com

Nan DeLuca is a full-time calligrapher in New York City. Her Web site includes samples of lettering styles, samples of her work, pricing information, a listing of services, and biographical information.

CyberScribes
http://www.calligraph.com/cyberscribes

CyberScribes is an online community of people dedicated to the art of calligraphy. Members can share contacts, tips, information about shows, workshops and
demonstrations, concerns, questions, and much more. Professionals and amateurs are welcomed.

Society of Scribes
PO Box 933
New York, NY 10150
(212) 452-0139
http://www.societyofscribes.org

A nonprofit educational organization that promotes the study, teaching, and practice of calligraphy and related disciplines.

CARICATURIST

National Caricaturist Network (NCN)
http://www.caricature.org

An international nonprofit organization dedicated to promoting the art of caricature, the education of the public and its members about the art form and profession, and assisting its members to secure group benefits. The NCN is a professional organization but welcomes anyone interested in the art of caricature. Associate and student memberships are available at a discounted rate for those who wish to simply be a part of the organization, or who want to learn more about becoming a professional caricaturist.

Caricature Connection
PO Box 692625
Orlando, FL 32869
(877) WE-DRAW-U
http://www.caricatureconnection.com

Web site filled with information about caricatures, hosted by caricaturist Keelan Parham, president of the National Caricaturist Network.

CATALOG COPYWRITER

Catalog Age
11 River Bend Drive South
PO Box 4242
Stamford, CT 06907-0242
http://multichannelmerchant.com/
contact/
Magazine dedicated to catalog production.

CLOTHING PATTERN MAKER

Cherie Bixler Pattern Service
http://www.theexecutivescloset.com/
cherie_bixler/services.htm
Professional business Web site for Cherie Bixler, pattern designer.

Council of Fashion Designers of America (CFDA)
1412 Broadway, Suite 2006
New York, NY 10018
(212) 302-1821
http://www.cfda.com
Founded in 1962, the CFDA works to advance the status of fashion design. It also sponsors the popular CFDA Fashions Awards, an event that is known as the Oscars of the fashion world. The organization includes more than 250 of the nation's best-known designers and others within the fashion industry.

COSTUME DESIGNER

Costume Designers Guild
4730 Woodman Avenue, Suite #430
Sherman Oaks, CA 91423
(818) 905-1557
cdgia@earthlink.net
http://www.costumedesignersguild.com

The Costume Designers Guild was founded in 1953 by a group of 30 motion picture costume designers. Today, its membership includes motion picture, television, commercial, and stage costume designers throughout the world and totals over 590 members. The Costume Designers Guild promotes the research, artistry, and technical expertise in the field of film and television costume design.

National Costumers Association
1265 W. Mountain View Drive
Mesa, AZ 85201
(800) NCA-1321
office@costumers.org
http://www.costumers.org

FINE ARTIST

Artist Directory
http://www.artistsguilds.com/directory.
htm
An online listing of about 30 art organizations, with links to each one. This diverse listing includes organizations such as the Smithsonian American Art Museum, the Nevada Camera Club, and the Art Dealers Association of America.

National Association of Independent Artists (NAIA)
http://www.naia-artists.org
An online site offering a wealth of information for fine artists of all types. Includes shows and contact information, classified ads, links to other sites, member rosters, and more.

FORENSIC ARTIST

American Academy of Forensic Sciences (AAFS)

PO Box 669
Colorado Springs, CO 80901-0669
(719) 636-1100
http://www.aafs.org

For more than 50 years the American Academy of Forensic Sciences (AAFS) has served a distinguished and diverse membership. With more than 5,600 members, the AAFS consists of 10 sections representing a wide range of forensic specialties, including artists, physicians, attorneys, dentists, toxicologists, physical anthropologists, document examiners, psychiatrists, engineers, criminalists, educators, and others who practice, study, and perform research in the forensic sciences. They represent all 50 states, Canada, and 50 other countries worldwide.

Artist Directory
http://www.artistsguilds.com/directory.htm

An online listing of about 30 art organizations, with links to each one. This diverse listing includes organizations such as the Smithsonian American Art Museum, the Nevada Camera Club, and the Art Dealers Association of America.

National Association of Independent Artists (NAIA)
http:/www.naia-artists.org

An online site offering a wealth of information for fine artists of all types. Includes shows and contact information, classified ads, links to other sites, member rosters, and more.

Scottsdale Artists' School
3720 North Marshall Way
Scottsdale, AZ 85251

(800) 335-5707
http://www.scottsdaleartschool.org

Offers basic and advanced courses in forensic art.

FURNITURE MAKER

The Furniture Society
Box 18
Free Union, VA 22940
(434) 973-1488
http://www.furnituresociety.org

A nonprofit organization whose mission is to advance the art of furniture making by inspiring creativity, promoting excellence, and fostering understanding of this art and its place in society.

Woodworker Online
http://www.woodworker-online.com

A woodworking resource for the craftsman, professional, hobbyist, and consumer.

GLASSBLOWER

Art Glass Association
(866) 301-2421
http://www.artglassassociation.com

A broad community of glass artists, retailers, commercial studios, material suppliers, publishers, designers, collectors, and hobbyists, all involved in a variety of art glass forms, including traditional stained glass, fused glass, blasted/carved glass, and lampworked glass.

GRAVESTONE CARVER

The Association for Gravestone Studies (AGS)

278 Main Street, Ste. 207
Greenfield MA 01301
(413) 772-0836
http://www.gravestonestudies.org

AGS was founded in 1977 for the purpose of furthering the study and preservation of gravestones. AGS is an international organization with an interest in gravemarkers of all periods and styles.

Karin Sprague Wood and Stone Carvers
904 Tourtellot Hill Road
No. Scituate, RI 02857
(401) 934-3105
http://www.karinsprague.com

The Web site features interviews with and descriptions of the works of gravestone carver Karin Sprague.

GREETING CARD WRITER

American Greetings Careers
http://careers.americangreetings.com
The careers Web site for American Greetings cards.

Greeting Card Association (GCA)
1156 15th Street, NW, Suite 900
Washington, DC 20005
(202) 393-1778
http://www.greetingcard.org

The trade organization representing greeting card and stationery publishers, and allied members of the industry. The organization's principal objectives are to promote the tradition of sending greeting cards, to represent the industry before government and regulatory agencies, to serve as an information service center for its members, and to monitor trends and developments that may impact the industry.

Hallmark Summer Internships
cstaff1@hallmark.com

E-mail this address if you're interested in learning more about summer internships at Hallmark.

HOLOGRAPHER

The Holographer Online Magazine
http://www.holographer.org

This site is for all those with an interest in display holography—the type of holograms intended for viewing directly, normally placed on a wall for display. It includes holograms of museum artifacts, art holography, and holographic portraiture.

JEWELRY DESIGNER

AJM Magazine, Education Guide
http://www.ajm-magazine.com

For information about jewelry-related certification programs.

California Institute of Jewelry Training
5800 Winding Way
Carmichael, CA 95608
(800) 731-1122
http://www.jewelrytraining.com

Institute that provides students the professionalism and skills for success in the jewelry industry as a designer, bench jeweler, stone setter, gemologist, or jewelry sales professional.

Center for Beadwork & Jewelry Arts
718 Thompson Lane, Suite 123
Nashville, TN 37204
(615) 292-0610
http://www.landofodds.com/beadschool/
studentguide/admin/careers.htm

The Center for Beadwork & Jewelry Arts was founded in 2000, and began offering classes in 2001. The CBJA is a school for beadwork and jewelry arts, providing elective and progressive track courses for students at all skill levels.

Gemological Institute of America (GIA)

5345 Armada Drive
Carlsbad, CA 92008
(800) 421-7250
http://www.gia.edu

Established in 1931, GIA is the world's largest nonprofit institute of gemological research and learning.

Jewelers of America

52 Vanderbilt Avenue, 19th Floor
New York, NY 10017
(800) 223-0673
http://www.jewelers.org

Jewelers of America is the national association for the retail jeweler.

Jewelry Design Institute

13354 Midlothian Turnpike, Suite 202
PO Box 475
Midlothian, VA 23113

Institute that provides students the skills for success as a designer in the jewelry industry.

Lapidary Journal

http://www.lapidaryjournal.com

This is the oldest gem and jewelry-making magazine in the world. Published 12 times a year, LJ covers a variety of topics in the area of gemcraft, jewelry making, and design. Each issue also includes a section of projects with step-by-step instructions.

Manufacturing Jewelers and Suppliers of America (MJSA)

45 Royal Little Drive
Providence, RI 02904
(800) 444-MJSA
http://www.mjsainc.com

A national association that represents the interests of those who are connected in any way to the manufacture or sale of jewelry.

KNITTING PATTERN DESIGNER

Crochet Guild of America (CGOA)

PO Box 3388
Zanesville, OH 43702-3388
(877) 852-9190 (free crochet help)
http://www.crochet.org

The Crochet Guild of America is a nonprofit organization, established with the purpose of preserving and advancing crochet. CGOA works to educate the public about crochet. They offer educational opportunities and networking for current crocheters. And they strive to raise the standards of the quality, art, and skill of crochet. Membership is open to anyone interested in crochet. Many knitters find crochet techniques useful and handy at times. The CGOA Web site offers online lessons (http://www.crochet.org/lessons/lesson.html) and they even operate a toll-free phone number you can call for help or advice. The Web site has a wealth of other information.

The Knitting Guild Association (TKGA)

PO Box 3388
Zanesville, OH 43702-3388
(740) 452-4541
TKGA@TKGA.com
http://www.tkga.com

The Knitting Guild Association offers numerous educational opportunities to its members. In addition to classes offered at the regional and national TKGA events, they offer many correspondence classes including Hand Knitting Basics, Basic, Basics; Professional Finishing, Master Hand Knitter (Levels I, II, and III), and much more. Membership in TKGA includes a subscription to the official TKGA publication Cast On.

The National NeedleArts Association (TNNA)

PO Box 3388
Zanesville, OH 43702-3388
(800) 889-8662
http://www.tnna.org

The National NeedleArts Association (TNNA) is an international trade organization. TNNA member businesses create and/or sell items related to the needle arts industry, which is made up primarily of needlepoint, cross-stitch, embroidery, knitting, and crochet. TNNA hosts three trade shows each year open only to member businesses. These trade shows allow pattern designers to check out the new yarns and trends in the industry. It also gives them the opportunity to network with yarn suppliers, other pattern writers, and other people in the needle arts industry.

Society of Craft Designers (SCD)

PO Box 3388
Zanesville, OH 43702-3388
(740) 452-4541
http://www.craftdesigners.org

The Society of Craft Designers was established in 1975 to represent the interests of craft designers throughout the industry. Today, its members include not only designers, but editors,
publishers, and manufacturers as well. The SCD offers members educational opportunities and networking opportunities. They also hold an annual professional conference with workshops and business seminars. An online newsletter keeps members up-to-date on the latest news and trends in the craft design industry. A mentor-mentee program helps new members learn about the SCD and the many opportunities it has to offer its members.

LAMPWORK BEAD ARTIST

Corning Museum of Glass

One Museum Way
Corning, NY 14830-2253
(800) 732-6845
http://www.cmog.org

The Corning Museum of Glass is home to the most comprehensive collection of glass in the world. In addition to the Sculpture Gallery and the Glass Collection Galleries with more than 3,500 years of glass, the museum has much more to offer both casual visitors and glass professionals. The Studio at the museum is an internationally renowned teaching facility offering a variety of programs—both residency and scholarship programs. The Studio also offers walk-in workshops, where visitors can try the art of hot glasswork, flamework, fusing, or sandblasting. The Rakow Research Library of the Corning Museum of Glass is "the world's foremost library on the art and history of glass and glassmaking."

Delphi Creativity Group

3380 East Jolly Road
Lansing, MI 48910
(800) 248-2048
http://www.delphiglass.com

Delphi is a large glass retailer located in Lansing, Michigan. They offer classes on many different facets of glass crafting, including lampwork.

The International Society of Glass Beadmakers (ISGB)
1120 Chester Avenue #470
Cleveland, OH 44114
(888) 742-0242
http://www.isgb.org

The International Society of Glass Beadmakers (ISGB) is a nonprofit organization dedicated to promoting and supporting the art of making handcrafted glass beads.

Lapidary Journal
60 Chestnut Avenue, Suite 201
Devon, PA 19333-1312
(610) 964-6300
http://www.lapidaryjournal.com

Lapidary Journal (LJ) is the oldest gem and jewelry-making magazine in the world. Published 12 times a year, LJ covers a variety of topics in the area of gemcraft, jewelry making, and design. Each issue also includes a section of projects with step-by-step instructions.

Step by Step Beads
60 Chestnut Avenue, Suite 201
Devon, PA 19333-1312
(800) 448-0865 (subscriptions only)
http://www.stepbystepbeads.com

Each issue of Step by Step Beads *contains instructions for 15 to 20 beads and beaded jewelry projects, at least one of which is a lampwork design. Recent issues have featured instructions for making lampwork Christmas stocking and elf boot beads, and lampwork conch shell beads, to name just a*

few. The Step by Step Beads Web site is a great source of information with sample projects, project reprints, bead classes, shops, societies, helpful beading links, and more.

WetCanvas!
http://www.wetcanvas.com

The glass art area at WetCanvas! (http://www.wetcanvas.com/forums/channels.php?s=&channel_id=40) is a great resource for lampwork bead artists. You can find news and articles, chat with other lampwork artists in the chat room, and exchange knowledge in the large forum. There are also many links of interest to glass artists.

LOGO DESIGNER

About.com: Graphic Design / About.com: Desktop Publishing
http://graphicdesign.about.com
http://desktoppub.about.com

Both the Graphic Design area and the Desktop Publishing area of About.com have lots of information related to logo design, including software and hardware, design tips, typography, fonts, education, employment, and freelancing. Each area also has numerous articles, tips, and more devoted to logo design. You can find them in the Graphic Design area at http://graphicdesign.about.com/od/logotips/index.htm and in the Desktop Publishing area at http://graphicdesign.about.com/od/logotips/index.htm.

Graphic Artists Guild
90 John Street, Suite 403
New York, NY 10038-3202
(212) 791-3400
http://www.gag.org

The Graphic Artists Guild is a national union of and for illustrators, Web designers, cartoonists, graphic designers, photographers, and other individuals working in similar creative areas. The Graphic Artists Guild publishes the Graphic Artists Guild Handbook of Pricing & Ethical Guidelines, *which contains information about working in the visual graphic arts field—everything from explanations of copyright law and other legal issues affecting graphic artists to tips on how to negotiate the best deal. The Graphic Artists Guild has nearly a dozen local chapters, which sponsor workshops and events, giving you an opportunity to network with other professionals in your area.*

MAKEUP ARTIST

Heather Fox, Makeup Artist
http://www.hfoxmakeup.com

Web site of Heather Fox, a makeup artist in Washington, D.C. It includes photos of her work, her resume, and the types of makeup services she provides.

The Studio Makeup Academy
1438 North Gower Street, #14
Hollywood, CA 90028
(323) 465-4002
http://www.studiomakeupacademy.com

Located within a film and television studio in Hollywood, the Studio Makeup Academy provides training in beauty makeup and film and television makeup. The classes are intended to prepare students for a career in the entertainment and beauty industries.

MURALIST

ArtLex Art Dictionary
http://www.artlex.com

An online dictionary defining more than 3,600 art-related terms, with pronunciation information, images, quotations, and cross-references. The site also includes more than 100 articles on a variety of art-related subjects.

National Society of Mural Painters
c/o American Fine Arts Society
215 West 57th Street
New York, NY 10019
http://www.anny.org/2/orgs/0041/mural.htm

The roots of the NSMP date back to 1895 when it was established as The Mural Painters. Today the organization works for the advancement of the techniques and standards for mural arts, as well as the design and actual painting of murals. Membership is open to muralists who have completed at least two full-sized mural pieces.

Painted House
http://www.painted-house.com

This is the Web site companion to Debbie Travis' Painted House (which airs on the Oxygen network). The site has directions for many of the projects featured on the shows more than 200 episodes. You can search the directions by techniques, which helps if you are looking for something specific. These directions cover a huge range of painting and faux finishing techniques—antiquing, combing, decoupage, faux brick, stenciling, stucco, and much, much more. A handy FAQ covers some of the more common painting questions and problems.

PACKAGE DESIGNER

Packaging Graphics
5732 Milentz Avenue
St. Louis, MO 63109
(314) 457-9095
http://www.packaginggraphics.net

A site for packaging designers that features an online newsletter called Packaging Designer News.

PHOTO RETOUCHER

An Interview With Glenn Honiball, Master Photo Retoucher
http://bermangraphics.com/press/retouch.htm

Larry Berman and Chris Maher of Berman Graphics interview Glenn Honiball, who has been a photo retoucher for more than 20 years and is known in the field as one of the best. The interview includes tips and suggestions from Honiball, as well as insights into how he works, the equipment he uses, and so forth.

POTTER

Nolde Forest Pottery
3401 New Holland Road
Mohnton, PA 19540
http://www.noldeforestpottery.com

Nolde Forest Pottery is the studio of Wesley Muckey and Greg Zieber, potters who specialize in traditional redware pottery. Their special interest is recreating historical styles of pottery. The Web site contains samples of their work, show information, and explanations of their works.

On-Line Arts & Crafts Movement Resource Directory

Chautauqua Publishing
2621 Clermont Street
Denver, CO 80207
(303) 388-2560
http://www.ragtime.org/Ragtime_Resources.html

An online directory of businesses, artists, antique dealers, and organizations related to the arts and crafts movement. Extensive resources for potters, including pottery artists and historic preservation organizations.

RESUME WRITER

National Resume Writers Association (NRWA)
PO Box 184
Nesconset, NY 11767
(631) 930-6287
http://www.nrwa.com/contact_nrwa.htm

Founded in 1997, the NRWA is a nonprofit, member-driven organization dedicated to promoting high standards of excellence through mentoring, education, and support services. NRWA has members from all over the United States, as well as Canada, Puerto Rico, Australia, Jamaica, and Brazil. Some members are home-based and others work from retail offices, some are full-time entrepreneurs, and others work part time. Members include writers, recruiters, counselors, and other employment and career-related professionals. The NRWA offers certification as an NCRW (Nationally Certified Resume Writer).

Professional Association of Resume Writers and Career Coaches (PARW/CC)
1388 Brightwaters Boulevard, NE

St. Petersburg, FL 33704
(800) 822-7279
http://www.parw.com

Founded in 1990, this association is dedicated to elevating the skills, credibility, visibility, and profitability of specialists in the fields of resume writing, career coaching, and career counseling. The international membership includes "retail" resume professionals and career coaches, career centers, career counselors, university placement personnel, government career counselors, recruiters, and job and career transition coaches. PARW/CC created the career industry's first certification program for resume professionals in 1991. Today, the Certified Professional Résumé Writer (CPRW) credential is the respected industry standard. The association helps resume writers and other career professionals exchange information, enhance their skills, or demonstrate their commitment to providing professional services to the general public. Association members include independent business owners, as well as nonprofit career centers such as colleges and universities, military bases, workforce development offices, and state Departments of Labor. Their participation in PARW/CC demonstrates an ongoing commitment to learning, exchanging ideas and information, and gaining the expertise to best help each client achieve their personal career goals.

SAND SCULPTOR

Sand Castle Central
http://www.sandcastlecentral.com

Sand Castle Central is a great source of information about sand sculpting. You'll find tips and tricks the pros use, information about tools, and lots of photos. There is a section where you can find out about upcoming sculpture contests, including those that allow amateurs to compete. You can also find contact information for professional sand sculptors, including those who give lessons.

Sculptor.org
309 North Virginia Avenue
Falls Church, VA 22046
http://www.sculptor.org

Sculptor.org is a huge Web site with over 400 pages and 12,000 links related to sculptors and sculpture. The site has sections for all sorts of different mediums, including sand (http://www. sculptor.org/Sculptors/sand.htm). In the sand sculptors or sculptures section, you'll find links to a number of different sculptors and sand sculpture companies. There are also links to other information related to sand sculpting.

World Sand Sculpting Academy (WSSA)
c/o Sand World International
PO Box 610
Solana Beach, CA 92075
(858) 847-0389
gkkirk@sandworld.com
http://www.wssa.info

The World Sand Sculpting Academy (WSSA), formerly known as the World Sand Sculpting Association, promotes sand sculpting as an internationally recognized profession and an art form. The WSSA has established standards, rules, and regulations for international competitions. They also serve as an international board of approval of sand sculpting events and competitions around the world.

World Championships of Sand Sculpture
info@harrisand.org
http://www.harrisand.org

The World Championships of Sand Sculpture begins each year on the Tuesday after Labor Day. The final judging takes place on Sunday afternoon. The finished sculptures are on display until Canadian Thanksgiving/Columbus Day in October.

STAINED GLASS ARTIST

Artists in Stained Glass (AISG)
RR #3
Scotch Line West
Minden, Ontario
Canada K0M 2K0
http://www.aisg.on.ca

Organization of stained glass artists, glass crafters, architects, hobbyists, and others interested in the development and promotion of stained glass as a contemporary art form. Members can include anyone who is interested in stained glass art, and who want the latest information on this art form, such as galleries, artists, architects, students, and teachers. The stained glass message board is a valuable free resource to exchange ideas, to look for employment or employees, to ask for help or information on stained glass techniques, to share one's expertise, and to discuss stained glass trends. The news page is open to all studios and stained glass artists (who have Web sites or e-mail) to publicize their stained glass workshops, lessons, or classes.

Glass Craftsman
Arts & Media, Inc.
10 Canal Street, Suite 300
Bristol, PA 19007
(215) 826-1799
http://www.glasscraftsman.com

National magazine for the stained glass artist, including articles about different stained glass artists, new products, and much more.

Crafts Report
100 Rogers Road
Wilmington, DE 19801-5041
(800) 777-7098
theeditor@craftsreport.com
http://www.craftsreport.com

Established in 1975, this is a monthly business magazine for the crafts professional, including articles on shows, health insurance, retirement planning, business issues, and much more.

Stained Glass Association of America
10009 East 62nd Street
Raytown, MO 64133
(800) 438-9581
http://www.stainedglass.org

The Stained Glass Association of America is a nonprofit association founded in 1903 to promote the development and advancement of the stained and decorative art glass craft. The association maintains the highest possible standards for excellence in craftsmanship, integrity, and business practices and tries to advance the awareness, understanding, appreciation, and potentialities of its craft and its organization. The group also offers guidelines, instruction and training to craftspersons and protects the craft against regulations restricting its freedom as an architectural art form.

The Stained Glass Quarterly
10009 East 62nd Street
Raytown, MO 64133
(800) 438-9581
http://www.stainedglass.org

An award-winning, four-color publication sent to all members of the Stained Glass Association of America.

TEXTILE DESIGNER

Nancy Eiseman Textile Designs
(610) 604-4930
nancy@nancyeiseman.com
http://nancy.eiseman.home.att.net

The Web site of freelance textile designer Nancy Eiseman, who also teaches at Philadelphia University, formerly known as Philadelphia College of Textiles and Science. The site contains samples from Eiseman's portfolio and information about her training and background.

The Textile Museum
2320 S Street, NW
Washington, DC 20008-4088
(202) 667-0441
http://www.textilemuseum.org

Founded in 1925 by George Hewitt Myers, the Textile Museum is housed in two buildings, one of which is Myers' former home. As one of the most specialized art museums in the country, the museum boasts 25,000 to 35,000 visitors a year. The museum includes a variety of permanent and changing exhibits.

VIDEO GAME DESIGNER

Sloperama Productions
PO Box 66640
Los Angeles, CA 90066
(310) 915-9945 (business calls only)
http://www.sloperama.com

A comprehensive Web site offering advice for those trying to get into the gaming industry, a history of the company, and much more.

VIOLIN MAKER

David T. Van Zandt, violin maker
1415 NW 70th Street
Seattle, WA
(206) 478-9603
dvz@vanzandtviolins.com
http://www.vanzandtviolins.com

The Web site of violin maker David T. Van Zandt, who makes Baroque, classical, and modern violins, violas, and cellos in his Seattle studio. His Web site includes photos of some instruments he's made, information about being a violin maker and how Van Zandt got into violin making, as well as links to other sites and an interview featuring Van Zandt.

The Violin Society of America (VSA)
48 Academy Street
Poughkeepsie, NY 12601
(845) 452-7557
http://www.vsa.to

The Violin Society of America was founded in 1974 and is open to anyone who has an interest in making or playing stringed instruments, or just shares a love of the instruments. The goal of the society is to promote the art and science of making, repairing, and preserving stringed musical instruments and their bows. The Web site includes information about conventions, competitions, and activities, as well as links to other organizations and information about the society.

WAX MUSEUM STUDIO ARTIST

Madame Tussaud New York
234 West 42nd Street
New York, NY 10036

info@madametussaudsny.com
http://www.nycwax.com/

Madame Tussaud's Wax Museum is a world-renowned institution featuring wax sculptures of a wide variety of well-known figures.

WEDDING GOWN DESIGNER

Council of Fashion Designers of America (CFDA)
1412 Broadway, Suite 2006
New York, NY 10018
(212) 302-1821
http://www.cfda.com

Founded in 1962, the CFDA works to advance the status of fashion design. It also sponsors the popular CFDA Fashions Awards, an event that is known as the Oscars of the fashion world. The organization includes more than 250 of the nation's best-known designers and other representatives of the fashion industry.

Foxglove Custom Bridal Gowns
South Strafford, VT 05070
(802) 765-4076
foxglove@valley.net
http://www.valley.net/~foxglove

This is the Web site of Rachel Kurland, a wedding gown designer in South Strafford, Vermont. The site contains samples of her work, an explanation of the process, and other information.

Philadelphia Fashion Coterie
55 North Third Street
Philadelphia, PA 19106
(215) 407-9903

A recently formed organization dedicated to helping designers and fashion retailers in the greater Philadelphia area, includ-ing southern New Jersey and Delaware. The group sponsors events to promote designers and retailers.

WINDOW DRESSER

Fashion Windows.Com, Inc.
PO Box 600632
Dallas, TX 75360
(214) 378-7192
http://www.fashionwindows.com

A Web site geared toward anyone interested in any aspect of the fashion industry, including window dressing. An entire section of the site is devoted to visual merchandising and includes interviews with window dressers, tips, and information.

WOOD-CARVER

Joe Leonard's Custom Wood Carving
12107 State Route 88
Garrettsville, OH 44231
(330) 527-2307
http://www.joeleonard.com

Joe Leonard is a master wood-carver, best known for his carousel horses. He also leads workshops and seminars. His work has been commissioned by clients from around the world. His Web site includes links to other wood carving sites, photos of his work, his biography, workshop listings, and more.

The National Wood Carvers Association (NWCA)
PO Box 43218
Cincinnati, OH 45243
http://www.chipchats.org

Started in 1953, the national association is best known for its bi-monthly maga-zine, Chip Chats. The magazine is trea-

sured by wood-carvers because of its useful information and resources. The organization has 46,000 members worldwide.

The Carvers' Companion

http://carverscompanion.com

A Web site committed to wood-carvers. Contains an online magazine for wood-carvers, sources for materials and supplies, a forum for communication between wood-carvers, and other features. Gives a look into the world of wood carving and wood-carvers.

Windsor Wood Carving Museum

850 Ouellette Avenue
Windsor, ON
Canada N9A 4M9
(519) 977-0823
http://www.windsorwoodcarving
museum.ca

The large, one-room museum exhibits traditional, contemporary, wildlife, and historical carvings, with new exhibits added each year. The museum contains about 150 carvings by noted artists, all displayed in glass cases in a climate-controlled environment.

YARN HAND-DYER

The Knitting Guild Association (TKGA)

PO Box 3388
Zanesville, OH 43702-3388
(740) 452-4541
tkga@tkga.com
http://www.tkga.com

Among the many classes taught at the regional and national Knitting Guild Association (TKGA) events, there is quite often at least one class on hand-dyeing yarn. In addition, every TKGA regional and national event features

a marketplace where hand-dyers can show off and sell their latest colors and colorways.

The National NeedleArts Association

PO Box 3388
Zanesville, OH 43702-3388
(800) 889-8662
http://www.tnna.org

The National NeedleArts Association (TNNA) is an international trade organization. TNNA members businesses create and/or sell items related to the needle arts industry, which is made up primarily of needlepoint, cross-stitch, embroidery, knitting, and crochet. TNNA hosts three trade shows each year open only to member businesses. These trade shows allow vendors, including yarn hand-dyers, to show off new products to the retailers attending the show. It also gives them the opportunity to network with other hand-dyers and other people in the needle arts industry.

PRO Chemical & Dye

PO Box 14
Somerset, MA 02726
(800) 228-9393
promail@prochemical.com
http://www.prochemical.com

PRO Chemical & Dye is the distributor of a wide variety of dyes, chemicals, textile paints, equipment, and related supplies. They offer a number of classes and workshops on various dyeing-related topics throughout the year. The Web site has a helpful product and use chart, a glossary for terms with which you might be unfamiliar, and an excellent article highlighting studio safety guidelines. PRO Chemical & Dye will help you with color matching by suggesting a starting formula free of charge.

APPENDIX B. ONLINE CAREER RESOURCES

This volume offers a look inside a wide range of unusual and unique careers that might appeal to someone with a creative spirit or personality. And while it highlights general information, it's really only a glimpse into the job. The entries are intended to merely whet your appetite, and provide you with some career options you may never have known existed.

Before jumping into any career, you'll want to do more research to make sure that it's really something you want to pursue. You'll most likely want to learn as much as you can about the careers in which you are interested. That way, as you continue to research and talk to people in those particular fields, you can ask informed and intelligent questions that will help you make your decisions. You might want to research the education options for learning the skills you'll need to be successful, along with scholarships, work-study programs, and other opportunities to help you finance that education. And, you might want answers to questions that were not addressed in the information provided here. If you search long enough, you can find just about anything using the Internet, including additional information about the jobs featured in this book.

✳**A word about Internet safety:** The Internet is a wonderful resource for networking. Many job and career sites have forums where students can interact with other people interested in and working in that field. Some sites even offer online chats where people can communicate with each other in real-time. They provide students and jobseekers opportunities to make connections and maybe even begin to lay the groundwork for future employment. But as you use these forums and chats, remember that anyone could be on the other side of that computer screen, telling you exactly what you want to hear. It's easy to get wrapped up in the excitement of the moment when you are on a forum or in a chat, interacting with people that share your career interests and aspirations. Be cautious about what kind of personal information you make available on the forums and in the chats; never give out your full name, address, or phone number. And never agree to meet with someone that you have met online.

SEARCH ENGINES

There are many search engines that will help you find out more about the jobs in this book and others that might interest you. And although you may have a favorite search engine, take some time to check out some of the others that are out there. Some have features that might help you find information not located with the others. Several engines will offer suggestions for ways to narrow your results, or related phrases you might want to search for along with your search results. This is handy if you are having trouble locating exactly what you want.

Another good thing to do is to learn how to use the advanced search features of your favorite search engines. Knowing that might help you to zero-in on exactly the information for which you are searching without wasting time looking through pages of irrelevant hits.

As you use the Internet to search information on the perfect career, keep in mind that, like anything you find on the Internet, you need to consider the source from which the information comes.

Some of the most popular Internet search engines are:

AllSearchEngines.com
http://www.allsearchengines.com
This search engine index has links to the major search engines along with search engines grouped by topic. The site includes a page with more than 75 career and job search engines at http://www.allsearchengines.com/careerjobs.html.

AlltheWeb
http://www.alltheweb.com

AltaVista
http://www.altavista.com

Ask Jeeves
http://www.ask.com

Dogpile
http://www.dogpile.com

Excite
http://www.excite.com

Google
http://www.google.com

HotBot
http://www.hotbot.com

LookSmart
http://www.looksmart.com

Lycos
http://www.lycos.com

Mamma.com
http://www.mamma.com

MSN Network
http://www.msn.com

My Way
http://www.goto.com

Teoma
http://www.directhit.com

Vivisimo
http://www.vivisimo.com

Yahoo!
http://www.yahoo.com

HELPFUL WEB SITES

The Internet has a wealth of information on careers—everything from the mundane to the outrageous. There are thousands, if not millions, of sites devoted to helping you find the perfect job for you and your interests, skills, and talents. The sites listed here are some of the most helpful ones that the authors came across and/or used while researching the jobs in this volume. The sites are listed in alphabetical order. They are offered for your information. The authors do not endorse any of the information found on these sites.

Absolute Arts
http://www.absolutearts.com
Absolute Arts is "the largest marketplace for contemporary art, art news, research, art gallery and artist portfolios, online since 1995." Artists can add their Web site to the online directory, participate in art discussion forums, learn more about art history (with the biographies of over 22,000 artists, and more than 200,000 images from museums), and more. You

can sign-up for the free e-mail newsletter *International Arts News* at the site.

All Experts

http://www.allexperts.com

"The oldest & largest free Q&A service on the Internet," AllExperts.com has thousands of volunteer experts to answer your questions. You can also read replies to questions asked by other people. Each expert has an online profile to help you pick someone who might be best suited to answer your question. Very easy to use, it's a great resource for finding experts who can help to answer your questions.

America's Career InfoNet

http://www.acinet.org

A wealth of information! You can get a feel for the general job market; check out wages and trends in a particular state for different jobs; learn more about the knowledge, skills, abilities, and tasks for specific careers; and learn about required certifications for specific careers and how to get them. You can search over 5,000 scholarship and other financial opportunities to help you further your education. A huge career resources library has links to nearly 6,500 online resources. And for fun, you can take a break and watch one of nearly 450 videos featuring real people at work: everything from custom tailors to engravers, glassblowers to silversmiths.

ArtCareer.net

http://www.artcareer.net

This Web site offers information on finding a job, a resume-posting option, career guidance, and more—a complete resource for careers in the visual arts.

Art Deadlines List

http://www.artdeadlineslist.com

For a small fee artists can get a monthly newsletter featuring 600 to 900 announcements (each month) listing contests, competitions, scholarships, grants, juried exhibitions, jobs, and much, much more. A small version of the newsletter highlighting 20 to 40 jobs is available for free. The Web site has an enormous section called Resources for Artists (http://artdeadlineslist.com/ar) with links for almost every imaginable art form. There is other useful information on the Web site like ideas for how to put your art on the Web, opportunity of the day, and more.

Art Schools

http://www.artschools.com

The Art Schools Web site offers a wealth of information about college degrees, programs, and workshops in all sorts of creative fields from traditional crafts such as ceramics and floral design, to the more unique like airbrushing, footwear design furniture design, and toy design. The site lists thousands of schools and workshops around the world. The site has lots of other information including articles on finding the right school for you, tips on applying, and information on financial aid. The majors/program section has a general description for many of the artistic specialties covered on the site, along with links for additional information. The careers/jobs area has articles and links to information on internships, the job search (art-focused), writing a resume and cover letters, and handling an interview. It even includes links and information for the self-employed artist. There are sections with links to news resources, and more. This is a do-not-miss site for anyone thinking about a career in the arts.

Artslynx
http://www.artslynx.org

Artslynx is a huge curated links library with resources for dance, theatre, visual arts, music, film, writing and poetry, arts education, employment, and much more.

Backdoor Jobs: Short-Term Job Adventures, Summer Jobs, Volunteer Vacations, Work Abroad and More
http://www.backdoorjobs.com

This is the Web site of the popular book by the same name, now in its third edition. While not as extensive as the book, the site still offers a wealth of information for people looking for short-term opportunities: internships, seasonal jobs, volunteer vacations, and work abroad situations. Job opportunities are classified into several categories: Adventure Jobs, Camps, Ranches & Resort Jobs, Ski Resort Jobs, Jobs in the Great Outdoors, Nature Lover Jobs, Sustainable Living and Farming Work, Artistic & Learning Adventures, Heart Work, and Opportunities Abroad.

Boston Works–Job Explainer
http://bostonworks.boston.com/globe/job_explainer/archive.html

For nearly 18 months, the Boston Globe *ran a weekly series profiling a wide range of careers. Some of the jobs were more traditional, but with a twist, like the veterinarian who makes house calls. Others were very unique and unusual, such as the profile of a Superior of Society monk. The profiles discuss an average day, challenges of the job, required training, salary, and more. Each profile gives an up-close and personal look at that particular career. In addition, the Boston Works Web site (http://bostonworks.boston.com) has a lot of good, general employment-related information.*

Career Guide to Industries
http://www.bls.gov/oco/cg/cgindex.htm

For someone interested in working in a specific industry, but maybe undecided about exactly what career to pursue, this site is the place to start. Put together by the U.S. Department of Labor, you can learn more about the industry, working conditions, employment, occupations (in the industry), training and advancement, earnings, outlook, and sources of additional information.

Career Planning at About.com
http://careerplanning.about.com

Like most of the other About.com topics, the career planning area offers a wealth of information, and links to other information on the Web. Among the excellent essentials are career planning A to Z, a career-planning glossary, information on career choices, and a free career-planning class. There are many great articles and other excellent resources.

Career Prospects in Virginia
http://www3.ccps.virginia.edu/career_prospects/default-search.html

Career Prospects is a database of entries with information about more than 400 careers. Developed by the Virginia Career Resource Network, the online career information resource of the

Virginia Department of Education, Office of Career and Technical Education Services, was intended as a source of information about jobs "important to Virginia," but it's actually a great source of information for anyone. While some of the information like wages, outlook, and some of the requirements may apply only to Virginia, the other information for each job (such as what it's like, getting ahead, skills) and the links will be of help to anyone interested in that career.

Career Voyages

http://www.careervoyages.gov

"The ultimate road trip to career success," sponsored by the U.S. Department of Labor and the U.S. Department of Education. This site features sections for students, parents, career changers, and career advisors with information and resources aimed to that specific group. The FAQ offers great information about getting started, the high-growth industries, how to find your perfect job, how to make sure you're qualified for the job you want, tips for paying for the training and education you need, and more. Also interesting are the Hot Careers and Emerging Fields sections.

Dream Jobs

http://www.salary.com/careers/
layouthtmls/crel_display_Cat10.html

The staff at Salary.com takes a look at some wild, wacky, outrageous, and totally cool ways to earn a living. The jobs they highlight include pro skateboarder, computer game guru, nose, diplomat, and much more. The profiles don't offer links or resources for more information, but they are informative and fun to read.

Find It! in DOL

http://www.dol.gov/dol/findit.htm

A handy source for finding information at the extensive U.S. Department of Labor Web site. You can search by broad topic category or by audience, which includes a section for students.

Fine Living: *Radical Sabbatical*

http://www.fineliving.com/fine/episode_
archive/0,1663,FINE_1413_14,00.
html#Series873

The show Radical Sabbatical on the Fine Living network looks at people willing to take a chance and follow their dreams and passions. The show focuses on individuals between the ages of 20 and 65 who have made the decision to leave successful, lucrative careers to start over, usually in an unconventional career. You can read all about these people and their journeys on the show's Web site.

Free Salary Survey Reports and Cost of Living Reports

http://www.salaryexpert.com

Based on information from a number of sources, Salary Expert will tell you what kind of salary you can expect to make for a certain job in a certain geographic location. Salary Expert has information on hundreds of jobs—everything from your more traditional white- and blue-collar jobs, to some unique and out of the ordinary professions like acupressurist, blacksmith, denture waxer, taxidermist, and many others. With sections covering schools, crime, community comparison, community explorer, and more, the Moving Center is a useful area for people who need to relocate for training or employment.

Fun Jobs

http://www.funjobs.com

Fun Jobs has job listings for adventure, outdoor, and fun jobs at ranches, camps, ski resorts, and more. The job postings have a lot of information about the position, requirements, benefits, and responsibilities so that you know what you are getting into ahead of time. And, you can apply online for most of the positions. The Fun Companies link will let you look up companies in an A-to-Z listing, or you can search for companies in a specific area or by keyword. The company listings offer you more detailed information about the location, types of jobs available, employment qualifications, and more.

Girls Can Do
http://www.girlscando.com

"Helping girls discover their life's passions," Girls Can Do has opportunities, resources, and a lot of other cool stuff for girls ages 8 to 18. Girls can explore sections such as Outdoor Adventure, Sports, My Body, The Arts, Sci-Tech, Change the World, and Learn, Earn, and Intern. In addition to reading about women in all sorts of careers, girls can explore a wide range of opportunities and information that will help them grow into strong, intelligent, capable women.

Global Art Information
http://www.globalartinfo.com

A subscription service listing thousands of competitions, grants, scholarships, residencies, internships, and more worldwide.

Global Art Jobs
http://www.globalartjobs.com

A subscription service listing art jobs worldwide. You will receive information about more than 1,500 jobs and opportunities each month with your subscription. In addition, you can list your resume on the site during your subscription period.

Great Web Sites for Kids
http://www.ala.org/gwstemplate.cfm?section=greatwebsites&template=/cfapps/gws/default.cfm

Great Web Sites for Kids is a collection of more than 700 sites organized into a variety of categories, including animals, sciences, the arts, reference, social sciences, and more. All of the sites included here have been approved by a committee made up of professional librarians and educators. You can even submit your favorite great site for possible inclusion.

Hot Jobs: Career Tools Home
http://www.hotjobs.com/htdocs/tools/index-us.html

While the jobs listed at Hot Jobs are more on the traditional side, the Career Tools area has a lot of great resources for anyone looking for a job. You'll find information about how to write a resume and a cover letter, how to put together a career portfolio, interviewing tips, links to career assessments, and much more.

Job Descriptions & Job Details
http://www.job-descriptions.org

Search for descriptions and details for more than 13,000 jobs at this site. You can search for jobs by category or by industry. You'd probably be hard-pressed to find a job that isn't listed here, and you'll probably find lots of jobs you never imagined existed. The descriptions and details are short, but it's interesting and fun, and might lead you to the career of your dreams.

Job Hunter's Bible
http://www.jobhuntersbible.com

This site is the official online supplement to the book What Color Is Your Parachute? A Practical Manual for Job-Hunters and Career-Changers, *and is a great source of information with lots of informative, helpful articles and links to many more resources.*

Job Profiles
http://www.jobprofiles.org

A collection of profiles where experienced workers share rewards of their job; stressful parts of the job; basic skills the job demands; challenges of the future; and advice on entering the field. The careers include everything from baseball ticket manager to pastry chefs and much, much more. The hundreds of profiles are arranged by broad category. While most of the profiles are easy to read, you can check out the How to browse JobProfile. org section (http://www.jobprofiles.org/ jphowto.htm) if you have any problems.

Major Job Web sites at Careers.org
http://www.careers.org/topic/01_jobs_ 10.html

This page at the Careers.org Web site has links for more than 40 of the Web's major job-related Web sites. While you're there, check out the numerous links to additional information.

Manhattan Arts International
http://www.manhattanarts.com

Manhattan Arts International is a career resource for artists. One of the main services offered by Manhattan Arts International is career consultation (for a fee). They also offer workshops and seminars, and a wealth of free information at their Web site. The magazine section has art and business articles, art and life essays, interviews, and exhibition reviews. There are multiple links to artist resources, which will be of interest and help to individuals in many different artistic fields, including juried exhibitions, professional services, organizations, books and periodicals, grants and funding, studios, and more. You can sign up for their free monthly newsletter, Art-E-News.

Monster Jobs
http://www.monster.com

Monster.com is one of the largest, and probably best known, job resource sites on the Web. It's really one-stop shopping for almost anything job-related that you can imagine. You can find a new job, network, update your resume, improve your skills, plan a job change or relocation, and so much more. Of special interest are the Monster: Cool Careers (http://change.monster.com/archives/coolcareers) and the Monster: Job Profiles (http://jobprofiles.monster. com) sections, where you can read about some really neat careers. The short profiles also include links to additional information. The Monster: Career Advice section (http://content.monster.com) has resume and interviewing advice, message boards where you can network, relocation tools and advice, and more.

Occupational Outlook Handbook
http://www.bls.gov/oco

Published by the U.S. Department of Labor's Bureau of Labor Statistics, the Occupational Outlook Handbook *(sometimes referred to as the* OOH*) is the premiere source of career information. The book is updated every two years, so you can be assured that the information you are using to help make your decisions is current. The online version is very easy to use; you can search for a specific occupation, browse though a group of related occupations, or look through an alphabetical listing of all the jobs included in the volume. Each of the entries highlights the general nature of the job, working conditions, training and other qualifications, job outlook, average earning, related occupations, and sources of additional information. Each entry covers several pages and is a terrific source to get some great information about a huge variety of jobs.*

The Riley Guide: Employment Opportunities and Job Resources on the Internet
http://www.rileyguide.com

The Riley Guide is an amazing collection of job and career resources. Unless you're looking for something specific, one of the best ways to maneuver around the site is with the A-to-Z Index. You can find everything from links to careers in enology to information about researching companies and employers. The Riley Guide is a great place to find just about anything you're looking for, and probably lots of things you never dreamed you wanted to know! But be forewarned—it's easy to get lost in the A-to-Z Index, because it's filled with so many interesting things.

Sculptor.org
http://www.sculptor.org

Sculptor.org is a huge Web site with over 400 pages and 12,000 links related to sculptors and sculpture. The site has sections for all different sorts of media, including soapstone, bronze, glass, pewter, ceramic, and wood, to name just a few. It also has sections for different types of sculptures including garden, religious, toy, wildlife, action figure, and more. In each section you'll find links to different sculptors, companies, and other resources related to that medium or type of sculpture. The site also has jobs and positions for sculptors; information about schools, workshops, foundations, grants, and scholarships; agents; studio opportunities; events and chats, magazines and journals; local and international organizations and associations; and much, much more.

USA TODAY Career Focus
http://www.usatoday.com/careers/dream/dreamarc.htm

USA TODAY *offers their "dream job" series on this Web site. In these interview profiles, people discuss how they got their dream job, what they enjoy the most about it, describe an average day, their education backgrounds, sacrifices they had to make for their jobs, and more. They also share words of advice for anyone hoping to follow in their footsteps. Most of the articles also feature links where you can find more information. The USATODAY.com Job Center (http://www.usatoday.com/money/jobcenter/front.htm) also has links to lots of resources and additional information.*

CAREER TESTS AND INVENTORIES

If you have no idea what career is right for you, there are many resources available online that you can use to categorize your interests and steer you in the right direction. While some of the assessments charge a fee, many others are free. You can locate more tests and inventories by searching for the keywords career tests, career inventories, or personality inventories. Some of the most popular assessments available online are:

Campbell Interest and Skill Survey (CISS)
http://www.usnews.com/usnews/edu/careers/ccciss.htm

Career Explorer
http://careerexplorer.net/aptitude.asp

Career Focus 2000 Interest Inventory
http://www.iccweb.com/careerfocus

Career Maze
http://www.careermaze.com/home.asp?licensee=CareerMaze

Career Tests at CareerPlanner.com
http://www.careerplanner.com

CAREERLINK Inventory
http://www.mpc.edu/cl/cl.htm

FOCUS
http://www.focuscareer.com

Keirsey Temperament Test
http://www.keirsey.com

Motivational Appraisal of Personal Potential (MAPP)
http://www.assessment.com

Myers-Briggs Personality Type
http://www.personalitypathways.com/type_inventory.html

Skills Profiler
http://www.acinet.org/acinet/skills_home.asp

The Career Interests Game
http://career.missouri.edu/students/explore/thecareerinterestsgame.php

The Career Key
http://www.careerkey.org

Princeton Review Career Quiz
http://www.princetonreview.com/cte/quiz/default.asp

APPENDIX C. ART SCHOOLS

In addition to these art colleges listed below, universities in almost every state have art departments and degrees in various art studies. Note: An asterisk (*) denotes a school also offering animation studies.

ALABAMA

Virginia College at Birmingham, Interior Design Programs*
65 Bagby Drive
Birmingham, AL 35209
(205) 802-1200
http://www.vc.edu

CALIFORNIA

The Art Institute of California–Los Angeles*
2900 31st Street
Santa Monica, CA 90405
(888) 646-4610
http://www.education.org/artinstitutes

California College of the Arts–Oakland
5212 Broadway
Oakland, CA 94618-1426
(800) 447-1ART
http://www.ccac-art.edu/

California College of the Arts–San Francisco
1111 Eighth Street
San Francisco, CA 94107-2247
(800) 447-1ART
http://www.ccac-art.edu/

The Fashion Institute of Design & Merchandising
919 South Grand Avenue
Los Angeles, CA 90015
(800) 624-1200
http://www.fidm.edu

Los Angeles Academy of Figurative Art
16926 Saticoy Street
Van Nuys, CA 91406
(818) 793-5063
http://www.laafigart.com

Otis College of Art and Design*
9045 Lincoln Boulevard
Los Angeles, CA 90045
(310) 665-6800
http://www.otis.edu

San Francisco Art Institute*
800 Chestnut Street
San Francisco, CA 94133
(415) 771-7020
http://www.sfai.edu/

COLORADO

The Art Institute of Colorado*
1200 Lincoln Street
Denver, CO 80203-2903
http://www.education.org/artinstitutes

Rocky Mountain College of Art & Design
1600 Pierce Street
Lakewood, CO 80214
(800) 888-ARTS
http://www.rmcad.edu

CONNECTICUT

Lyme Academy College of Fine Arts
84 Lyme Street
Old Lyme, CT 06371
(860) 434-5232
http://www.lymeacademy.edu

DELAWARE

Delaware College of Art and Design*
600 North Market Street

Wilmington, DE 19801
(302) 622-8000
http://www.dcad.edu/

FLORIDA

Digital Media Arts College
3785 North Federal Highway
Boca Raton, FL 33431
(866) 255-3622
http://www.education.org/dmac

Florida School of the Arts
5001 St. Johns Avenue
Palatka, FL 32177
(386) 312-4300
http://www.floarts.org

**Miami International University of Art &
Design***
1737 North Bayshore Drive
Miami, FL 33132
(305) 995-5000
http://www.education.org/artinstitutes

The Art Institute of Fort Lauderdale*
1799 Southeast 17th Street
Fort Lauderdale, FL 33316
(800) 275-7603
http://www.education.org/artinstitutes

The Art Institute of Tampa*
Parkside at Tampa Bay Park
4401 North Himes Avenue, Suite 150
Tampa, FL 33614-7001
(866) 703-3277
http://www.education.org/artinstitutes

GEORGIA

The Art Institute of Atlanta *
6600 Peachtree Dunwoody Road
Atlanta, GA 30328
(800) 275-4242
http://www.education.org/artinstitutes

Atlanta College of Art
Woodruff Arts Center
1280 Peachtree Street, NE
Atlanta, GA 30309
(800) 832-2104
http://www.aca.edu

Portfolio Center*
125 Bennett Street, NW
Atlanta, GA 30309-1268
(800) 255-3169
fernando@portfoliocenter.com
http://www.portfoliocenter.com

Savannah College of Art and Design*
PO Box 3146
22 East Lathrop Avenue
Savannah, GA 31402-3146
(800) 869-7223
http://www.scad.edu/

ILLINOIS

American Floral Art School
634 South Wabash Avenue # 210
Chicago, IL 60605
(312) 922-9328

The American Academy of Art
332 South Michigan Avenue, Suite 300
Chicago, IL 606041
(888) 461-0600
http://www.aaaart.edu

Harrington College of Design
200 West Madison Street, 2nd Floor
Chicago, IL 60606-3433
(877) 939-4975

The Illinois Institute of Art Chicago*
350 North Orleans, Suite 136-L
Chicago, IL 60654-1593
(800) 351-3450
http://www.education.org/artinstitutes

**International Academy of Design &
Technology**
One North State Street, Suite 400

Chicago, IL 60602
(312) 980-9200
http://www.iadtchicago.edu

School of the Art Institute of Chicago*
37 South Wabash Avenue
Chicago, IL 60603-3103
(312) 899-5219
admiss@artic.edu
http://www.artic.edu/saic

LOUISIANA

Baton Rouge Fine Arts Academy
2834 South Sherwood Forest Boulevard
Baton Rouge, LA 70816
(225) 295-1644
noart@msn.com
http://members.cox.net/larrycasso/index.htm

MAINE

Center for Furniture Craftsmanship
25 Mill Street
Rockport, ME 04856
(207) 594-5611
http://www.woodschool.org

Haystack Mountain School of Crafts
PO Box 518
Deer Isle, ME 04627
(207) 348-2306
http://www.haystack-mtn.org

Heartwood College of Art
123 York Street
Kennebunk, ME 04043
(207) 985-0985
http://www.heartwoodcollegeofart.org

Maine College of Art
97 Spring Street
Portland, ME 04101
(800) 639-4808
http://www.meca.edu

Portland Pottery Inc
118 Washington Avenue

Portland, ME 04104
(800) 539-4301
http://www.portlandpottery.com

MARYLAND

Baltimore Clayworks
5707 Smith Avenue
Baltimore, MD 21209
(410) 578-1919
http://www.baltimoreclayworks.org

Baltimore School For The Arts
712 Cathedral Street
Baltimore, MD 21201
(410) 625-0403
http://www.bsfa.org/index2.html

The Schuler School of Fine Arts
5 East Lafeyette Avenue
Baltimore, MD 21202
(410) 685-3568
http://www.auronet.com/schuler/index.html

Maryland College of Art and Design
10500 Georgia Avenue
Silver Spring, MD 20902
(301) 649-4454
http://www.mcadmd.org

Maryland Institute College of Art
1300 Mount Royal Avenue
Baltimore, MD 21217
(410) 669-9200
http://www.mica.edu

MASSACHUSETTS

The Art Institute of Boston at Lesley University*
700 Beacon Street
Boston, MA 02215
(800) 773-0494 ext. 6700
http://www.aiboston.edu

Boston Architectural Center, College of Architecture and Interior Design Programs
320 Newbury Street

Boston, MA 02115
(877) 585-0100
admissions@the-bac.edu
http://www.the-bac.edu

Boston Arts Academy
174 Ipswich Street
Boston, MA 02215
(617) 635-6470
http://boston.k12.ma.us/baa

Butera School of Art*
111 Beacon Street
Boston, MA 02116
(617) 536-4623
signs@butera.com
http://www.buteraschool.com

Cape Cod School of Art
48 Pearl Street
PO Box 948
Provincetown, MA 02657
(508) 487-0101
http://www.capecodschoolofart.com/
pages/study.html

Eliot School of Fine and Applied Arts
PO Box 351
24 Eliot Street
Jamaica Plain, MA 02130
(617) 524-3313
http://www.eliotschool.org

Massachusetts College of Art
621 Huntington Avenue
Boston, MA 02115
(617) 879-7000
http://www.massart.edu

Montserrat College of Art
PO Box 26
23 Essex Street
Beverly, MA 01915
(800) 836-0487
http://www.montserrat.edu

The New England Institute of Art (Boston)*
10 Brookline Place West
Brookline, MA 02445
(800) 903-4425
http://www.education.org/artinstitutes

MICHIGAN

Center for Creative Studies*
201 East Kirby Street
Detroit, MI 48202
(313) 664-7400
admissions@ccscad.edu
http://www.ccscad.edu

Cranbrook Academy of Art
39221 Woodward Avenue
PO Box 801
Bloomfield Hills, MI 48303-0801
(877) GO-CRANBrook
http://www.cranbrook.edu/art

Interlochen Center for the Arts
PO Box 199
Interlochen, MI 49643
(231) 276-7472
http://www.interlochen.org

Kendall College of Art and Design
Ferris State University
17 Fountain Street
Grand Rapids, MI 49503
(800) 676-2787
http://www.kcad.edu

MINNESOTA

The Art Institutes International Minnesota*
15 South 9th Street
Minneapolis, MN 55402-3137
(800) 777-3643
http://www.education.org/artinstitutes

Academy College Of Digital Art and Design*

1101 East 78th Street, Suite 100
Bloomington, MN 55420
(800) 292-9149
http://www.academycollege.edu

College of Visual Arts
344 Summit Avenue
St. Paul, MN 55102
(800) 224-1536
http://www.cva.edu

Minneapolis College of Art & Design*
2501 Stevens Avenue South
Minneapolis, MN 55404
(800) 874-MCAD
http://www.mcad.edu

MISSISSIPPI

Covenant School For The Arts
4000 Ridgewood Road
Jackson, MS 39211
(601) 981-9406

MISSOURI

Kansas City Art Institute*
4415 Warwick Boulevard
Kansas City, MO 64111
(800) 522-5224
http://www.kcai.edu

NEVADA

The Art Institute of Las Vegas*
2350 Corporate Circle
Henderson, NV 89074
(800) 833-2678
http://www.education.org/artinstitutes

International Academy of Design and Technology–Las Vegas
2495 Village View Drive
Henderson, NV 89074
(866) 400-4238

NEW HAMPSHIRE

Great River Arts Institute
PO Box 639
Walpole, NH 03608
(603) 756-3638
http://www.greatriverarts.org

NEW JERSEY

Guild of Creative Art
620 Broad Street
Shrewsbury, NJ 07702
(732) 741-1441
guildofcreativeart@att.net
http://www.guildofcreativeart.com

Joe Kubert School of Cartoon and Graphic Art
37 Myrtle Avenue
Dover, NJ 07801
(973) 361-1327
http://www.kubertsworld.com

Mid-Atlantic Regional School of Photography
Grand Hotel
Cape May, NJ
(888) 267-MARS
http://www.photoschools.com

NEW MEXICO

La Puerta Azul Art School
PO Box 2611
73 Sugar Lane
Taos, NM 87571
(505) 758-5180
http://www.lapuertaazulartschool.com

Albuquerque Artist's Academy
13307 Sunset Canyon Drive NE
Albuquerque, NM 87111
(505) 271-1035

Albuquerque School, Fine Arts
873 Tramway Lane Court NE

Albuquerque, NM 87122
(505) 856-5159

Art Center Design College–Albuquerque*
5000 Marble NE
Albuquerque, NM 87110
(800) 825-8753
http://www.theartcenter.edu

Center For Indigenous Arts & Culture
PO Box 8627
Santa Fe, NM 87504
(505) 473-5375
public44.freeyellow.com/indig.html

Institute of American Indian Arts
PO Box 20007
Sante Fe, NM 87504
(505) 424-2300
http://www.iaiancad.org/academic_
programs.htm

Poeh Arts Program
78 Cities Of Gold Road
Santa Fe, NM 87506
(505) 455-1110
http://www.poeharts.com

Printmaking Center at the College of Santa Fe
1600 Saint Michaels Drive
Santa Fe, NM 87505
(505) 473-6564
http://www.printmakingcenter.com

Santa Fe Art Institute
1600 St Michael's Drive
Santa Fe, NM 87505
(505) 424-5050
http://www.sfai.org/index2.html

Santa Fe Clay
1615 Paseo de Peralta
Santa Fe, NM 87501
(505) 984-1122
http://www.santafeclay.com

Santa Fe School for the Arts
5912 Jaguar Road

Santa Fe, NM 87507
(505) 438-8585
http://www.santafeschoolforthearts.com

Santa Fe School of Weaving
614 Paeso de Peralta
Santa Fe, NM 87501
(505) 982-6312
http://www.sfschoolofweaving.com/
classes.html

Taos Art School
PO Box 2588
Taos, NM 87571
(505) 758-0350
http://www.taosartschool.org

Taos Institute of Arts
108 Civic Plaza Drive
Taos, NM 87571
(800) 822-7183
http://www.taosnet.com/TIA

NEW YORK

American Handweaving Museum and Thousand Islands Craft School—Art Workshop
314 John Street
Clayton, NY 13624
(313) 686-4123
http://www.thousandisland.com/ahmtics

The Art Institute of New York City
75 Varick Street (One Hudson Square)
16th Floor
New York, NY 10013
(800) 654-2433
http://www.education.org/artinstitutes

Art League of Long Island
330 Cuba Hill Road
Huntington, NY 11743
(631) 368-0018
http://www.artleagueli.org

Art Muse—George Eastman House, Photography Programs

1114 Avenue Of The Americas
New York, NY 10036
(212) 857-0000
http://www.photomuse.org/indexIE.html

Art Students League of New York
215 West 57th Street
New York, NY 10019
(212) 247-4510
http://www.theartstudentsleague.org

Bridgeview School of Fine Arts
42-26 28th Street
Second Floor
Long Island City, NY 11101
(718) 937-1300
http://www.academicart.com

Chambers Pottery Inc.
153 Chambers Street
New York, NY 10007
(212) 619-7302
http://www.chamberspottery.com

Cooper Union for the Advancement of Science and Art
30 Cooper Square
New York, NY 10003
(212) 353-4120
http://www.cooper.edu/art/Welcome.html

Doll Artisan Guild School of Dollmaking
PO Box 1113
118 Commerce Road
Oneonta, NY 13820
(607) 432-4977
http://www.dollartisanguild.org

Fashion Institute of Technology, State University of New York*
Seventh Ave at 27th Street
New York, NY 10001-5992
(212) 217-7999
http://www.fitnyc.edu

Folk Art Institute of the Museum of American Folk Art
West 62nd Street

New York, NY 10023-7015
(212) 977-7298
http://www.folkartmuseum.org/afam_frames.asp?platform=win&browser=ie&ver=6

Island Drafting & Technical Institute, CADD Program
128 Broadway
Amityville, NY 11701
(631) 691-8733
http://www.islanddrafting.com

Parsons School of Design
66 Fifth Avenue
New York, NY 10011
(212) 229-8900
http://www.parsons.edu/

Pratt Institute
200 Willoughby Avenue
Brooklyn, NY 11205
(718) 636-3600
http://www.pratt.edu
         or
144 West 14th Street
New York, NY 10011
(212) 647-7775

Puerto Rican Workshop Inc./aka: Taller Boricua*
1680 Lexington Avenue
New York, NY 10029
(212) 831-4333
http://www.tallerboricua.org

School of Visual Arts*
209 East 23rd Street
New York, NY 10010
(212) 592-2100
http://www.schoolofvisualarts.edu/main.html

Sotheby's Institute of Art–New York
1334 York Avenue
New York, NY 10021
(212) 894-1111
http://search.sothebys.com

OHIO

Columbus College of Art & Design
107 North Ninth Street
Columbus, OH 43215
(614) 224-9101
http://www.ccad.edu

OREGON

Pacific Northwest College of Art
1241 Northwest Johnson Street
Portland, OR 97209
(503) 226-4391
http://www.pnca.edu

PENNSYLVANIA

Moore College of Art & Design
20th Street and The Parkway
Philadelphia, PA 19103-1179
(800) 523-2025
http://www.moore.edu

The Pennsylvania Academy of Fine Arts
School of Fine Arts
118 North Broad Street
Philadelphia, PA 19102
(215) 972-7600
http://www.pafa.org

Pennsylvania College of Art & Design
204 North Prince Street
PO Box 59
Lancaster, PA 17608-0059
(717) 396-7833
http://www.pcad.edu

RHODE ISLAND

Rhode Island School of Design*
2 College Street
Providence, RI 02903
(401) 454-6100
http://www.risd.edu

SOUTH CAROLINA

School of the Building Arts, Inc.
Old City Jail
20 Franklin Street
Charleston, SC 29401
(877) 283-5245
http://www.aboutsoba.org

Thornwell School For The Arts
604 East Home Avenue
Hartsville, SC 29550
(843) 383-3127
http://www.darlington.k12.sc.us/
dcsdweb/profiles/TES/index.html

TENNESSEE

Arrowmont School of Arts and Crafts
556 Parkway
Gatlinburg, TN 37738
(865) 436-5860
http://www.arrowmont.org

International Academy of Design and
Technology–Nashville
1 Bridgestone Park
Nashville, TN 37214

Memphis College of Art
1930 Poplar Avenue
Overton Park
Memphis, TN 38104
(800) 727-1088
http://www.mca.edu

Nossi College of Art
907 Two Mile Parkway, Suite E6
Goodlettsville, TN 37072
(615) 851-1088
http://www.nossi.com

Watkins College of Art & Design
2298 MetroCenter Boulevard
Nashville, TN 37228
(615) 383-4848
http://www.watkins.edu

TEXAS

Art Center Of Cedar Park
108 Raley Road
Cedar Park, TX 78613
(512) 259-0303
http://dragonflypond.net

The Art Institute of Dallas
2 North Park, 8080 Park Lane
Dallas, TX 75231-9959
(800) 275-4243
http://www.Education.org/artinstitutes

Ava Everett-Glass Fusing
3205 Dagan Drive
Plano, TX 75023
(972) 618-4135

Bee Cave Art School
15740 Hamilton Pool Road
Austin, TX 78735
(512) 263-0138
http://home.austin.rr.com/tntintx/BCAS.html

Caddo Lake Photographic Workshops
506 Private Road 2422
Uncertain, TX 75661
(903) 679-3154
http://www.caddolakephoto.com

Cotton Mary Art Academy
1511 Baggett Lane
Houston, TX 77055
(713) 957-1168
maryecotton@sbcglobal.net

Craft Guild Of Dallas
14325 Proton Road
Dallas, TX 75244-3512
(972) 490-0303
http://www.craftguildofdallas.com

Creative Arts Center of Dallas, Inc.
2360 Laughlin Drive
Dallas, TX 75228-6841
(214) 320-1275
http://www.creativeartscenter.org

Gemini School of Visual Arts & Communication
501 Prize Oaks Drive
Cedar Park, Williamson, TX 78613
(512) 249-1237
info@geminischool.com
http://www.geminischool.com

Glassell School Of Art
5101 Montrose Boulevard
Houston, TX 77006
(713) 639-7500
http://www.mfah.org/main.asp?target=destination2&par1=1

Glassworks
2503 Montrose Boulevard
Houston, TX 77006
(713) 524-8455

VERMONT

Fletcher Farm School for the Arts & Crafts
611 Route 103 South
Ludlow, VT 05149
(802) 228-8770
http://www.fletcherfarm.com

Frank Covino Academy of Art
Mt. Ellen Village, Sugarbush Valley
Waitsville, VT 05673-0420
(802) 496-2513
http://www.portrait-art.com

Springhouse School of the Arts*
206 Commerce Street
Hinesburg, VT 05461
(802) 482-2840
http://www.springhousearts.com

VIRGINIA

The Art Institute of Washington
1820 North Fort Myer Drive
Arlington, VA 22209
(703) 358-9552
http://www.education.org/artinstitutes

WASHINGTON

The Art Institute of Seattle
2323 Elliot Avenue
Seattle, WA 98121-1622
(800) 275-2471
http://www.education.org/artinstitutes

Corbin Art Center
507 West 7th Avenue
Spokane, WA 99204
(509) 625-6677
http://www.spokanecity.org/parks/
corbin/index.htm

Cornish College of the Arts
1000 Lenora Street
Seattle, WA 98121
(800) 726-ARTS
http://www.cornish.edu

Coupeville Arts Center
15 Northwest Birch Street
Coupeville, WA 98239
(360) 678-3396
http://www.coupevillearts.org

Kirkland Arts Center, Visual Arts School
620 Market Street
Kirkland, WA 98033-5421
(425) 822-7161
http://www.kirklandartscenter.org/
classes.html

Mariah Art School
410 Jefferson Street SE # 9
Olympia, WA 98501
(360) 357-9188

Mesmer Animation Labs*
1116 Northwest 54th Street, Suite A
Seattle, WA 98107
(206) 782-8004
http://www.mesmer.com

Monart School of Art–Bainbridge Island
11290 A Sunrise Drive
Bainbridge Island, WA 98110

(360) 662-1542
http://www.kitsapart.com/index.html

Pilchuck Glass School
315 Second Avenue South, Suite 200
Seattle, WA 98104-2618
(206) 621-8422
http://www.pilchuck.com

Pratt Fine Arts Center
1902 South Main Street
Seattle, WA 98144-2206
(206) 328-2200
http://www.pratt.org

Roaring Mouse Creative Arts
9559 Sandpoint Way NE
Seattle, WA 98115
(206) 522-1187
http://www.roaringmouse.org

School of Visual Concepts
500 Aurora Avenue North
Seattle, WA 98109
(206) 623-1560
http://www.schoolofvisualconcepts.com

Sculptor's Workshop
700 Main Street
Edmonds, WA 98020
(425) 774-8282

Spokane Art School
920 North Howard Street
Spokane, WA 99201
(509) 328-0900
http://www.spokaneartschool.org

WASHINGTON, DC

Corcoran College of Art & Design–Downtown Campus
500 17th Street, NW
Washington, DC 20006
(202) 639-1801
http://www.corcoran.edu

Corcoran College of Art & Design–Georgetown Campus

1801 35th Street, NW
Washington DC   20007
(202) 298-2540
http://www.corcoran.edu

WEST VIRGINIA

**International Academy of Design and
Technology–Fairmont**
2000 Green River Drive
Fairmont, WV 26554

WISCONSIN

Glass Garden Studio, Art Classes
724 East South Street
Beaver Dam, WI 53916
(920) 885-9881

Interior Garden Art Studio
100 South Main Street
Thiensville, WI 53092
(262) 238-1804

Lake Country Fine Arts
112 West Capitol Drive
Hartland, WI 53029
(262) 367-2900

Madison Creative Art Program
3200 Monroe Street
Madison, WI 53711
(608) 238-7641
http://www.madcap.org

Madison Media Institute
One Point Place, Suite 1
Madison, WI 53719
(800) 236-4997
http://www.madisonmedia.com

Milwaukee Institute of Art and Design
273 East Erie Street
Milwaukee, WI 53202
(414) 291-8070
http://www.miad.edu/

Monroe Street Fine Arts Center
2526 Monroe Street
Madison, WI 53711
(608) 232-1510
http://www.msfac.org

Peninsula Art School of Door County
3906 County Road F, PO Box 304
Fish Creek, WI 54212-0304
(920) 868-3455
http://www.peninsulaartschool.com

WYOMING

Yellowstone Institute
PO Box 117
Yellowstone Park, WY 82190
(307) 344-2294
http://www.yellowstoneassociation.org/

READ MORE ABOUT IT

The following sources and books may help you learn more about creative careers.

GENERAL

Brabec, Barbara. *Creative Cash: How to Profit From Your Special Artistry, Creativity, Hand Skills, and Related Know-How.* Philadelphia: Three Rivers Press, 1998.

Gulrich, Kathy. *187 Tips for Artists: How to Create a Successful Art Career—and Have Fun in the Process!* New York: Center City Publishing, 2003.

Kadubec, Phil. *Crafts and Craft Shows: How to Make Money.* New York: Watson-Guptill Publications, 2000.

Landman, Sylvia. *Crafting for Dollars: Turn Your Hobby into Serious Cash.* New York: Prima Lifestyle, 1996.

Michels, Carroll. *How to Survive and Prosper as an Artist: Selling Yourself Without Selling Your Soul.* 5th ed. New York: Owl Books, 2001.

ANIMATOR

Colonna, Phyllis, and Della Mae Rasmussen. *The Power of Dreaming: Featuring the Story of Walt Disney.* Antioch, Calif.: Eagle Systems International Publication, 1981.

Parham, Keelan. *Let's Toon Caricatures.* Orlando, Fla.: Lunar Donut Press, 2003.

Silver, Stephen. *The Art of Silver.* Los Angeles: Silvertoons, 2004.

ARCHITECTURAL ILLUSTRATOR

Doyle, Michael E. *Color Drawing: Design Drawing Skills and Techniques for Architects, Landscape Architects, and Interior Designers.* Hoboken, N.J.: John Wiley and Sons, Inc., 1999.

Lin, Mike W. *Drawing and Designing with Confidence: A Step by Step Guide.* Hoboken, N.J.: John Wiley and Sons, Inc. 1997.

ART CONSERVATOR

James, Philip, and Sarah Batiste, eds. *Curators & Collections: Conservation of the Arts.* London: CV Publications, 1999.

Oddy, Andrew, ed. *The Art of the Conservator.* Washington, D.C.: Smithsonian Institution Press, 1992.

Price, Nicholas Stanley; M. Kirby Talley, Jr.; and Alessandra Melucco Vaccaro, eds. *Historical and Philosophical Issues in the Conservation of Cultural Heritage.* Los Angeles: Getty Conservation Institute, 1996.

ART DEALER

Bailey, Emma. *Sold to the Lady in the Green Hat.* New York: Dodd, Mead, 1962.

Brémond d'Ars, Yvonne de. *In the Heart of Paris: The Adventures of an Antique Dealer.* New York: Putnam, 1960.

Feigen, Richard. *Tales from the Art Crypt: The Painters, the Museums, the Curators, the Collectors, the Auctions, the Art.* New York: Knopf, 2000.

Klein, Ulrike. *The Business of Art Unveiled: New York Art Dealers Speak Up.* New York: Peter Lang Publishing, 1994.

BALLOON SCULPTURE ARTIST

Captain Visual. *The Big Book of Balloons: Create Almost Anything for Every Party and Holiday*. Secaucus, N.J.: Carol Pub. Group, 1998.

———. *Captain Visual's Big Book of Balloon Art! A Complete book of Balloonology for Beginners and Advanced Twisters*. Secaucus, N.J.: Carol Pub. Group, 1996.

Hardy, Marvin L. *Balloon Magic*. Wichita, Kans.: Pioneer Balloon Co., 2001.

Levine, Shar, and Michael Ouchi. *The Ultimate Balloon Book: 46 Projects to Blow Up, Bend & Twist*. New York: Sterling Pub., 2001.

Somekh, Addi, and Charlie Eckert. *The Inflatable Crown Balloon Hat Book*. San Francisco: Chronicle Books, 2001.

BOARD GAME DESIGNER

Buchanan, Ben, Carol J. Adams, and Susan Allison. *Journey to Gameland: How to Make a Board Game from your Favorite Children's Book*. New York: Lantern Books, 2001.

Levy, Richard, and Ronald O. Weingartner. *Toy and Game Inventor's Handbook*. Indianapolis, Ind.: Alpha, 2003.

Loader, Jeff, and Jennie Loader. *Making Board, Peg & Dice Games*. Lewes, U.K.: Guild of Master Craftsman Publications, 1993.

BOOKBINDER

Loudon, J. H. *James Scott and William Scott, Bookbinders*. London: Scolar Press in association with the National Library of Scotland, 1980.

BUMPER STICKER WRITER

Glatzer, Jenna. *Sell The Fun Stuff: Writers' And Artists' Market Guidelines For Greeting Cards, Posters, Rubber Stamps, T-shirts, Aprons, Bumper Stickers, Doormats, And More!* Available online at http://www.absolutewrite.com/ebook store/index.htm.

Miller-Louden, Sandra. *A Few, Choice Words: Short, Do-Able Writing That Sells*. Pittsburgh, Pa.: Jam Packed Press, 2000. Also available on-line at http://www.greetingcardwriting.com.

———. *Write Well and Sell: Greeting Cards*. Pittsburgh, Pa.: Jam Packed Press, 1998. Also available online at http://www.greetingcardwriting.com.

Wigand, Molly. *How to Write and Sell Greeting Cards, Bumper Stickers, T-Shirts and Other Fun Stuff*. Cincinnati, Ohio: F&W Publications, 1992.

CALLIGRAPHER

Shepherd, Margaret. *Learn Calligraphy: The Complete Book of Lettering and Design*. New York: Broadway Books, 2001.

Young, Caroline, and Chris Lyon. *Calligraphy: From Beginner to Expert*. Tulsa, Okla.: Usborne Books, 1994.

CARICATURIST

Hughes, Alex. *Caricatures*. New York: HarperCollins, 1999.

Parham, Keelan. *Let's Toon Caricatures*. Orlando, Fla.: Lunar Donut Press, 2003.

Redman, Lenn. *How to Draw Caricatures*. New York: McGraw-Hill, 1984.

CATALOG COPYWRITER

Bly, Robert. *The Copywriter's Handbook: A Step-By-Step Guide To Writing That Sells*. New York: Henry Holt, 1990.

Lewis, H.G. *Catalog Copy That Sizzles*. New York: McGraw-Hill, 1999.

Sroge, Maxwell. *How To Create Successful Catalogs*. New York: McGraw-Hill, 1995.

Werz, Edward, and Sally Germain. *Phrases That Sell: The Ultimate Phrase Finder to Help You Promote Your Products,*

Services, and Ideas. New York: McGraw-Hill, 1998.

CLOTHING PATTERNMAKER

Armstrong, Helen Joseph. *Patternmaking for Fashion Design.* Upper Saddle River, N.J.: Pearson Education, 1999.

Bergh, Rene. *Make Your Own Patterns: An Easy, Step-by-Step Guide to Making Over 60 Patterns.* London: New Holland Publishers, UK Limited, 1997.

COSTUME DESIGNER

Chiericehetti, David. *Edith Head: The Life and Times of Hollywood's Celebrated Costume Designer.* New York: HarperCollins, 2003.

Holkeboer, Katherine. *Patterns for Theatrical Costumes: Garments, Trims, and Accessories from Ancient Egypt to 1915.* London: Drama Publishers, 1993.

Kidd, Mary T. *Stage Costume Step-By-Step: The Complete Guide to Designing and Making Stage Costumes for All Major Drama Periods and Genres from Classical Through the Twentieth Century.* Cincinnati, Ohio: F & W Publications, 1996.

LaMotte, Richard E. *Costume Design 101: The Art and Business of Costume Design for Film and Television.* Studio City, Calif.: Michael Wiese Productions, 2001.

Pecktal, Lynn. *Costume Design: Techniques of Modern Masters.* New York: Watson-Guptill Publications, 1999.

FINE ARTIST

Grant, Daniel. *The Fine Artist's Career Guide.* 2nd ed. New York: Allworth Press, 2004.

FORENSIC ARTIST

Camenson, Blythe. *Opportunities in Forensic Science Careers.* New York: McGraw-Hill, 2001.

Gibson, Lois, and Deanie Francis Mills. *Faces of Evil: Kidnappers, Murderers, Rapists and the Forensic Artist Who Puts Them Behind Bars.* East Rutherford, N.J.: New Horizon Press Publishers, 2005.

Inde, Vilis. *Art in the Courtroom.* Westport, Conn.: Praeger Publishers, 1998.

Lang, Cay. *Taking the Leap: Building a Career as a Visual Artist.* San Francisco: Chronicle Books, 1998.

Taylor, K.T. *Forensic Art and Illustration.* Boca Raton, Fla.: CRC Press LLC, 2001.

FURNITURE DESIGNER

Grant, Daniel. *The Fine Artist's Career Guide.* 2nd ed. New York: Allworth Press, 2004.

Jackson, Albert. *The Complete Manual of Woodworking.* New York: Knopf, 1997.

Nagyszalanczy, Sandor. *Setting Up Shop: The Practical Guide to Designing and Building Your Dream Shop.* Newtown, Conn.: Taunton Press, 2001.

Rae, Andy. *The Complete Illustrated Guide to Furniture and Cabinet Construction.* Newtown, Conn.: Taunton Press, 2001.

Stankus, Bill. *How to Design and Build Your Ideal Woodshop.* Cincinnati, Ohio: Popular Woodworking Books, 2001.

GLASSBLOWER

Giberson, Dudley. *A Glassblower's Companion: A Compilation of Studio Equipment Designs, Essays, & Glassblowing Ideas.* Warner, N.H.: Joppa Glassworks Inc, 1998.

Schmid, Edward. *Beginning Glassblowing.* Bellingham, Wash.: Glass Mountain Press, 1998.

GRAVESTONE CARVER

Chase, Theodore, and Laurel Gabel. *Gravestone Chronicles II: More Eighteenth-Century New England Carvers and an Exploration of Gravestone Heraldica.* Boston: New England Historic Genealogical Society, 1997.

GREETING CARD WRITER

Miller-Louden, Sandra. *Write Well and Sell: Greeting Cards.* Pittsburgh, Pa.: Jam Packed Press, 1998. Also available online at http://www.greetingcardwriting.com.

Moore, Karen Ann. *You Can Write Greeting Cards.* Cincinnati, Ohio: Writer's Digest Books, 1999.

HOLOGRAPHER

Hariharan, P. *Optical Holography: Principles, Techniques and Applications.* Cambridge: Cambridge University Press, 1996.

———. *Basics of Holography.* Cambridge: Cambridge University Press, 2002.

Kasper, Joseph, and Steven Feller. *The Complete Book of Holograms: How They Work and How to Make Them.* Mineola, N.Y.: Dover Publications, 2001.

Lang, Cay. *Taking the Leap: Building a Career As a Visual Artist.* San Francisco: Chronicle Books, 1998.

Rhody, Alan. *Holography Market Place.* 8th ed. Berkeley, Calif.: Ross Books, 1999.

JEWELRY DESIGNER

Knuth, Bruce. *Jeweler's Resource: A Reference of Gems, Metals, Formulas and Terminology for Jewelers.* Rev. ed. Thornton, Colo.: Jewelers Press; 2000.

McCreight, Tim. *Jewelry: Fundamentals of Metalsmithing.* Cincinnati, Ohio: North Light Books, 1997.

McGrath, Jinks. *The Encyclopedia of Jewelry-Making Techniques: A Comprehensive Visual Guide to Traditional and Contemporary Techniques.* Philadelphia: Running Press, 1995.

Olver, Elizabeth. *Jewelry Making Techniques Book: Over 50 Techniques for Creating Eyecatching Contemporary and Traditional Designs.* Cincinnati, Ohio: North Light Books, 2001.

von Neumann, Robert. *The Design and Creation of Jewelry.* Iola, Wisc.: Krause Publications, 1982.

KNITTING PATTERN DESIGNER

Budd, Ann. *The Knitter's Handy Book of Patterns: Basic Designs in Multiple Sizes & Gauges.* Loveland, Colo.: Interweave Press, 2002.

Newton, Deborah. *Designing Knitwear.* Newtown, Conn.: Taunton Press, 1998.

Square, Vicki. *The Knitter's Companion.* Loveland, Colo.: Interweave Press, 1996.

Walker, Barbara G. *A Second Treasury of Knitting Patterns.* Pittsville, Wisc.: Schoolhouse Press, 1998.

———. *A Treasury of Knitting Patterns.* Pittsville, Wisc.: Schoolhouse Press, 1998.

Wiseman, Nancie. *The Knitter's Book of Finishing Techniques.* Woodinville, Wash.: Martingale, 2002.

Zimmermann, Elizabeth. *Elizabeth Zimmerman's Knitting Workshop.* Pittsville, Wisc.: Schoolhouse Press, 1981.

———. *Knitting Without Tears: Basic Techniques and Easy-to-Follow Directions for Garments to Fit All Sizes.* New York: Simon & Schuster, 1973.

LAMPWORK BEAD ARTIST

Jenkins, Cindy. *Beads of Glass.* Oak Park, Ill.: Pyro Press, 2003.

———. *Making Glass Beads.* Asheville, N.C.: Lark, 2004.

Kervin, James. *More Than You Ever Wanted to Know about Glass Beadmaking.* Livermore, Calif.: GlassWear Studios, 1999.

Tettinger, Corina. *Passing the Flame: A Beadmaker's Guide to Detail and Design.* 2nd ed. Friday Harbor, Wash.: Bonzobucks & Books, 2002.

MAKEUP ARTIST

Aucoin, Kevyn. *The Success, Struggles and Beauty Secrets of a Legendary Makeup Artist.* New York: Atria Books, 2003.

Brown, Bobbi, and Annemarie Iverson. *Bobbi Brown Beauty.* New York: HarperCollins Publishers, 1998.

MURALIST

Lord, Gary, and David Schmidt. *Marvelous Murals You Can Paint.* Cincinnati, Ohio: North Light Books, 2001.

Pittman, Rebecca. *How to Start a Faux Painting or Mural Business: A Guide to Making Money in the Decorative Arts.* New York: Allworth Press, 2003.

PACKAGE DESIGNER

Carter, David E. *Big Book of Design Ideas.* New York: HarperCollins Publishers, 2003.

PHOTO RETOUCHER

Eismann, Katrin, and Doug Nelson. *Photoshop Restoration & Retouching.* 2nd ed. Indianapolis, Ind.: New Riders Publishing, 2003.

POTTER

Mattison, Steve. *The Complete Potter.* Hauppauge, N.Y.: Barron's Educational Series, Inc., 2003.

Peterson, Susan. *The Craft and Art of Clay: A Complete Potter's Handbook.* New York: The Overlook Press, 2003.

RESUME WRITER

Enelow, Wendy. *Resume Winners from the Pros: 177 Of the Best from the Professional Association of Resume Writers.* Manassas Park, Va.: Impact Publications, 1998.

Whitcomb, Susan Britton. *Resume Magic: Trade Secrets of a Professional Resume Writer.* 2nd edition. Indianapolis, Ind.: JIST Works, 2003.

SAND SCULPTOR

Siebert, Ted. *The Art of Sandcastling.* Seattle, Wash.: Romar Books, 1990.

Wierenga, Lucinda. *The S.o.B. "take me to the beach" Sand Castle Book.* South Padre Island, Tex.: Sons of the Beach, 1999.

Wierenga, Lucinda, and Walter McDonald. *Sand Castles, Step-by-Step.* New York: Simon & Schuster, 1990.

STAINED GLASS ARTIST

Daley, Patricia Ann. *Stained Glass: Step by Step.* Hand Books Press, 2003.

Isenberg, Anita, and Seymour Isenberg. *How to Work in Stained Glass.* Iola, Wisc.: Krause Publications, 1998.

Wardell, Randy. *Introduction to Stained Glass: A Teaching Manual.* Ft. Lauderdale, Fla.: Wardell Publications, 2000.

TEXTILE DESIGNER

Meller, Susan. *Textile Designs: Two Hundred Years of European and American Patterns Organized by Motif, Style, Color, Layout, and Period.* New York: Harry N. Abrams, Inc., 2002.

VIDEO GAME DESIGNER

Laramee, Francois Dominic. *Game Design Perspectives.* Hingham, Mass.: Charles River Media, 2002.

Marley, Phil. *How to Get a Fab Job as a Video Designer*. Calgary, Alberta: FabJob.com, 2003.

VIOLIN MAKER

Bachman, Alberto Abraham, and Albert E. Weir. *Encyclopedia of the Violin*. Cambridge, N.Y.: Da Capo Press, 1975.

Ossman, Bruce. *Violin Making: A Guide for the Amateur*. East Petersburg, Pa.: Fox Chapel Publishing Company, Inc., 1997.

WAX MUSEUM STUDIO ARTIST

Bloom, Michelle. *Waxworks: A Cultural Obsession*. Minneapolis: University of Minnesota Press, 2003.

Pilbeam, Pamela. *Madame Tussaud and the History of Waxworks*. London: Hambledon & London, 2003.

Miller, Richard McDermott. *Figure Sculpture in Wax and Plaster*. Mineola, N.Y.: Dover Publications, 1987.

WEDDING GOWN DESIGNER

Andriks, Susan E. *Bridal Gowns: The Basics of Designing, Fitting and Sewing Your Wedding Dress*. Portland, Ore.: Palmer-Pletsch Associates, 1999.

Khalje, Susan. *Bridal Couture: Fine Sewing Techniques for Wedding Gowns and Evening Wear*. Iola, Wisc.: Krause Publications, 1997.

WINDOW DRESSER

Doonan, Simon. *Confessions of a Window Dresser: Tales from a Life in Fashion*. New York: Studio, 1998.

WOOD-CARVER

Bull, Graham R. *The Complete Woodcarver's Handbook*. Bethel, Conn.: Cambium Books, 2002.

Bridgewater, Alan and Gill. *Woodcarving Basics*. New York: Sterling Publishing Co., Inc., 2002.

Horner, Ken. *Woodworker's Essential Facts, Formulas & Short-Cuts: Rules of Thumb Help Figure It Out, With or Without Math*. Bethel, Conn.: Cambium Books, 2003.

YARN HAND-DYER

Blumenthal, Betsy, and Kathryn Kreider. *Hands on Dyeing*. Loveland, Colo.: Interweave Press, 1988.

Klos, Dagmar. *The Dyer's Companion*. Loveland, Colo.: Interweave Press, 2004.

Menz, Deb. *Color Works: The Crafter's Guide to Color*. Loveland, Colo.: Interweave Press, 2004.

Milner, Ann. *The Ashford Book of Dyeing*. Rev. ed. Petaluma, Calif.: Unicorn, 1998.

Potter, Cheryl, and Alexis Xenakis. *Handpaint Country: A Knitter's Journey*. Sioux Falls, S.Dak.: XRX Books, 2002.

INDEX